Teac

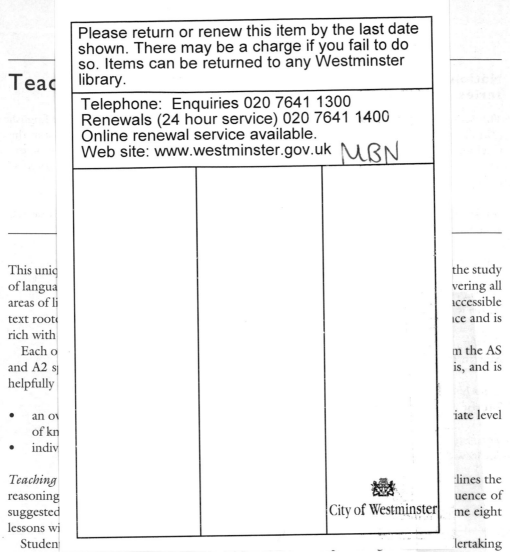

This uniq .... the study
of langua .... vering all
areas of li .... accessible
text root .... ce and is
rich with

Each o .... m the AS
and A2 s .... is, and is
helpfully

- an ov .... iate level
  of kn
- indiv

Teaching .... lines the
reasoning .... uence of
suggested .... me eight
lessons wi

Studen .... lertaking
the teaching of language for the first time, will welcome this highly practical resource.

Martin Illingworth is a consultant teacher with the National Association for the Teaching of English and works at Woodlands School in Derby and at The University of Nottingham, UK.

Nick Hall is East Midlands Regional Director at *Teach First*, and was previously Head of English and an Advanced Skills Teacher at Woodlands School, Derby, UK.

National Association for the Teaching of English (NATE) series

This series of books co-published with the National Association for the Teaching of English (NATE) reflects the organisation's dedication to promoting standards of excellence in the teaching of English, from early years through to university level. Titles in this series promote innovative and original ideas that have practical classroom outcomes and support teachers' own professional development.

Books in the NATE series include both pupil and classroom resources and academic research aimed at English teachers, students on PGCE/ITT courses and NQTs.

Titles in this series include:

International Perspectives on Teaching English in a Globalised World
Andrew Goodwyn, Louann Reid and Cal Durrant

Teaching English Language 16–19
Martin Illingworth and Nick Hall

Unlocking Poetry (CD-ROM)
Trevor Millum and Chris Warren

Teaching English Literature 16–19
Andrew Green, Gary Snapper and Carol Atherton

Teaching English Language 16 – 19

A comprehensive guide for teachers of AS/ A2 level English Language

Martin Illingworth and Nick Hall

Routledge
Taylor & Francis Group

LONDON AND NEW YORK

NATE

First published 2013
by Routledge
2 Park Square, Milton Park, Abingdon, Oxon OX14 4RN

Simultaneously published in the USA and Canada
by Routledge
711 Third Avenue, New York, NY 10017

Routledge is an imprint of the Taylor & Francis Group, an informa business

British Library Cataloguing in Publication Data
A catalogue record for this book is available from the British Library

Library of Congress Cataloging in Publication Data
Illingworth, Martin.
Teaching English language 16-19 : a comprehensive guide for teachers of AS/
A2 level English language / authored by Martin Illingworth and Nick Hall.
p. cm.
Includes index.
ISBN 978-0-415-52824-5 -- ISBN 978-0-415-52825-2 -- ISBN 978-0-203-
11854-2 1. English language--Study and teaching. 2. English teachers--Training
of. I. Hall, Nick. II. Title.
PE1065I46 2012
428.00712--dc23
2012017672

ISBN: 978-0-415-52824-5 (hbk)
ISBN: 978-0-415-52825-2 (pbk)
ISBN: 978-0-203-11854-2 (ebk)

Typeset in Galliard
by Saxon Graphics Ltd, Derby

MIX
Paper from
responsible sources
FSC® C004839
www.fsc.org

Printed and bound in Great Britain by
TJ International Ltd, Padstow, Cornwall

Contents

Figures and tables

Frontispiece: The Wedding Guest being prevented by the Ancient Mariner from attending the wedding, scene from 'The Rime of the Ancient Mariner', by S. T. Coleridge, published by Harper & Sons, New York, 1876 (wood engraving), Doré, Gustave (1832–83)/private collection/The Bridgeman Art Library.

Preface

We need to make school interesting and fulfilling. The way to do this is to make it relevant to the lives that the students are living. Incessant short-term worrying about examination results is stultifying and counter-productive to what really matters: *developing the learning capabilities of the young people in our charge.* We do not know what demands the future will bring; so we need to build into our educational processes the idea that what we are doing is developing capacity within our students to be able to approach any situation that befalls them in the future with a sense of confidence, resilience and resourcefulness. Schools have had a tendency to build a curriculum around content and its regurgitation when what is called for is a set of skills to deal with the unknown challenges ahead. Develop in the student these abilities and they will be able to deal with the shorter-term challenge of the examination system. Please don't base your learning environment around the needs of exams but around the real needs of the learner.

In this book of ideas that supports the teaching of A level English Language, we hope to empower teachers new to the course with the base knowledge and confidence to allow their students to explore and investigate the English language. Here we give you many ideas on how to design, structure and present your course so that the student takes ownership of the learning.

A level English Language is a growth subject and one that every teacher of English should enjoy teaching.

Martin Illingworth and Nick Hall

Source: Gustav Doré, *Plate 2: The Wedding Guest*, from 'The Rime of the Ancient Mariner', by S.T. Coleridge, published by Harper & Sons, New York, 1876 (wood engraving). Doré, Gustave (1832–83)/private collection/The Bridgeman Art Library.

How we have organised the book

Each of the chapters in this book is either an examined area of study from the AS and A2 syllabuses or deals with the supporting frameworks of linguistic analysis.

Each chapter consists of two main elements:

* An overview of that section which indicates our philosophy on how to teach that area of study and a discussion of the appropriate level of knowledge that the student will require; and
* Individual lesson ideas and plans, with resources.

Chapter 1: An introductory sequence of lessons

This section outlines the reasoning behind our investigative approach to the study of language. A sequence of suggested lesson ideas for the opening lessons of your course, amounting to some eight lessons with homework research and discussion preparation tasks, is included.

The rest of the book is organised into the following chapters.

Chapter 2: Audience, purpose and context

Each of the individual frameworks outlined in Chapter 3 below is only of value in relation to *audience, purpose and context*. In assessing speech and writing and also in producing it, a student must always consider the make-up of audiences, potential purposes of the language, and the needs of context.

Chapter 3: General frameworks

At AS and A2 level, the relevant frameworks are *grammar, lexical choices (vocabulary), semantics (the study of meaning), pragmatics (social and psychological features of interactions), discourse (structure), register/phonology and graphology (presentational features in writing)*.

* We consider each of the frameworks, providing an introductory commentary discussing appropriate levels of demand that should be placed upon students, valuing an investigative rather than didactic approach.

- There are also exemplar materials that include modelled annotations to help in the shaping and leading of discussion work.
- We also include some thinking around the idea that language has built-in redundancy.

Chapter 4: Conventions of written and spoken texts

One way to challenge the popular notion that writing is in some way superior to speech is to highlight the distinctive nature of and subtlety of spoken expression, by making use of transcripts recorded in differing contexts. A consideration of internet chat, a hybrid form of communication, would allow you and your class to reflect upon the constituent parts of each form of communication and their relative appropriate contexts. Also included in this chapter are some lessons that look at specific instances of spoken language in everyday usage.

Chapter 5: Language in society

- *Gender variations*: this is a very popular area for students to investigate. We consider here research techniques that will allow students to investigate for themselves the ways in which gender seems to impact on the way that we employ speech. There will be an opportunity to 'measure' raw data that your students collect against theoretical analyses.
- *The role language plays in demonstrating power*: making use of political and legal environments to view formal situations in which power is asserted alongside more 'everyday' transcripts.
- *How technology is impacting upon language change*: an area of study close to the hearts of A level students! It is also a fast changing area that teachers need to keep up to date with. Much that is printed about this area is obsolete. Therefore, we would suggest that you, once again, take an investigative approach to studying this area. The student that collects, for instance, all of their incoming text messages for a fortnight will have very 'real' and immediate data with which to study patterns and trends in the discourse features of that mode of communication.

Chapter 6: Original writing

In *original writing* coursework, students have to produce pieces of creative writing for real audiences and real purposes. In this section we provide good examples of productive choices and strong presentational methods. The students choose their own topics and forms but they will need to be guided by you.

Chapter 7: Language change

Here we provide you with an overview of the history of the English language and of the key players and events that trace the development of the language.

Hopefully, we shall also instil the idea that language evolves as a means of expression for the people that use it and that it is merely a reflection of those people and the world that they need to describe. It is important to note the ways in which people have resisted change and to make sure that teachers and students wishing to be accurate observers of language describe what they see rather than make judgements about those language choices.

The importance of context when analysing a text is particularly stressed by exam boards, and we would hope to support you to train your students to be alert to the fact that a text is merely one artefact from a time and place that does not necessarily represent all texts of that date.

Genres develop and it can be interesting to trace their development. In this section we give some useful examples.

Chapter 8: Language acquisition

This area of study covers two broad areas:

- the development of speech, from birth through the 'critical' period up to around four years of age; and
- debates around the learning of reading and writing.

Some theory is required, and provided here, to give your students an understanding of the stages that development goes through. However, again, the exam boards are clear on the importance of an informed investigation routed in examination of transcripts of children in real situations employing language for real purposes.

Chapter 9: Language investigation

In *investigative coursework*, students choose an area of the course that has interested them and conduct a short research project. They pose themselves a question that they do not know the answer to, collect data and analyse the patterns and trends that they discover making use of the linguistic frameworks that they have been introduced to. Your guidance is extremely important throughout the project, from shaping the question, considering the collection of 'fair' data, developing methods of analysis, to the organisation of the final folder. In this section we provide support for you in how to organise folders and some strong examples of productive and popular areas of study.

Chapter 1

An introductory sequence of lessons

To begin your course, you need to start to develop in your linguists an enquiring mind. You will find that the students in front of you probably take most language for granted most of the time. Opening their eyes to the complexity and subtlety of language transaction is important if they are to gain an understanding of how language works.

Here is our suggestion of how to approach the course.

Ask yourself the following question.

"What will the children in the classrooms of today need to know in 15 years' time?"

Uhm! It is a rapidly changing world and the rate of that change is surely only going to increase. The O level that I gained in 1984 in Computer Studies has become a most useless and obsolete qualification.

The answer to the question may well be that we do not really know what it is that they will need to know. This, then, presents us with a problem. What shall we teach them? If times change and conventional wisdom cannot keep up, then is it impossible to prepare students for what lies ahead?

Perhaps one answer lies in the word *prepare*. We cannot know what needs to be known but we can help students gain the skills of interpretation, judgement and analysis. If our students can *understand* the world around them, then they will be better equipped to deal with whatever is in front of them. They shall be prepared.

English Language A level is all about our constantly changing modes of communication. Indeed, it focuses entirely upon the ways that we express ourselves. Language changes because we have new things to describe, our society moves forward in its thinking and the experiences that we encounter need a voice. Language is one force that can keep up with change. It is a reflection of our world and changes because we change.

English Language is a growth A level, perfectly suited to the needs of providing valid modern educational experience. It is about our experiences of life and how we characterise those experiences through words. Sometimes we are simply communicating facts and opinions. However, we use language in so many other ways: to express emotion; to make 'small talk' creating a sense of comfort; for the sheer pleasure of making a noise; to make information permanent for generations to come; to make life seem quantifiable and 'real'; as an instrument of thought; and as a means of creating an identity. Language is a complex, sophisticated structure that we take for granted most of the time.

At its core, English Language A level allows students to investigate the language choices that they make individually and that we have collectively agreed upon. An appreciation of the workings of language and the purposes for which it can be employed can be an invaluable tool in facing that unknowable future.

The aim of this book is to help the teacher of A level English Language. There are two distinct objectives that we have in mind. First, we wish to put forward a distinctive approach to teaching English at advanced level which makes use of investigative approaches that will create thoughtful and self-reliant pupils capable of evaluating, analysing and producing language. Secondly, we hope to produce lots of practical ideas to support the investigative approach to study. A little base knowledge is required and this will be outlined under the individual component units.

It is important that students become alert to the ways that language is being employed around them if they are to develop linguistic skills. You are looking to make them into people that question and evaluate the language choices that they encounter in their everyday lives. Resources for you to investigate can very easily come from the students themselves. You will know that your students are developing in their linguistic awareness when they start to volunteer examples of language use that they have found interesting or articles that relate to the area that you are considering. To create resource banks collectively is extremely helpful, not only in providing data for analysis but in helping to give a sense of ownership of the course over to the students.

Stimulating interest in language exploration at the beginning of the course does not require reference to textbooks full of technical vocabulary and research. Indeed, that sort of approach can seem dry and somewhat daunting. To write down *Semantics* and be told that it means the study of meaning is, I would contend, meaningless. To investigate the ways that actual texts create meaning, exploring the different shades of meaning that words and phrases can have for different audiences, in differing contexts, when writers or speakers have differing purposes, makes the process of discovering a much clearer and meaningful experience. Understanding gained in this way can be transferred across texts and situations and will form the basis of good practice in a student's approach to study. At this stage of the course, you may well be consulting theoretical textbooks to support your presentation of ideas but it is texts and transcripts that you need to be working on with students.

Activities to stimulate linguistic exploration

1. How meanings are created

Take this very simple example of wordplay.

> I ordered two chocolate éclairs!

First, you could try to work out the context of this utterance. Where would such an utterance take place? Who might the speakers be? Perhaps the group will agree that the words come from a conversation between a diner and a waiter in a restaurant. This is plausible. You could then discuss the nature of the utterance. It is interesting that these words lend themselves to a certain context. You could explore the whole area of language that is context-bound, i.e. it could only be spoken in a particular set of circumstances or only retains its meaning in a particular situation.

Are the words rude? Polite? What relationship do these words have with what goes before or after? Is there a general script or framework within which speakers stay in certain contexts?

Do the diner and the waiter have a general understanding of the shape that their conversation will follow?

You could examine the possible ways there are of uttering these words. If you place emphasis on different words within the sentence here, the meaning is entirely changed. If we agree that the waiter has brought the wrong order to the table, the placing of the emphasis will alert the waiter to the nature of his mistake.

I ordered two chocolate éclairs!

Here, it seems that the waiter has placed the dessert in front of the wrong person.

I ordered two chocolate éclairs!

Now, the waiter has brought the wrong number of éclairs to the table.

I ordered two chocolate éclairs!

Whoops! The waiter has brought strawberry éclairs to the table.

I ordered two chocolate éclairs!

This time, the waiter has brought two chocolate doughnuts. Oh dear!

I ordered two chocolate éclairs!

The creation of meaning with this emphasis is not quite so certain. It may be a general statement of frustration or annoyance. It may be an implied comment that no éclairs have arrived at all. This raises the idea that emphasis might not always be making meaning clear.

Of course, the way that the words are uttered will have an impact upon the creation of meaning. Said with a 'smile' in the voice, then the speaker will indicate that this error has not really upset them. Again here, there is a whole range of possibilities.

In working on this utterance, pupils can appreciate that meaning is not just about words and sequences of words. The situation is far more subtle than that. Spoken texts have the added nuance of the mode of transmission, namely, speech and the contextual factors and frameworks that surround the conversation.

2. Relationships between words

The English language has always absorbed words from the other languages that it has come into contact with. It has also 'imported' words from certain fields and created new lexical items in this way. Twenty years ago a dictionary would have told us that 'mobile' is a noun referring to a suspended toy in a young child's bedroom or a qualifying adjective, as in the phrase 'mobile home'. Now, the same word has a new, perhaps more widely used function as a lexical item meaning 'mobile phone'. Indeed, our language has gained much of its expressive power from having a number of ways of saying the same thing. Words in isolation, however, do not really mean very much.

Investigate the word *hello*. What does it mean? It is difficult to say what it means. It is easy to give an example of it in use and to identify the purpose to which it is put. It is a far harder task to develop a definition of its meaning.

Ask the pupils to draw the word *road*. Look at all the drawings and then tell them that road was only part of a compound noun and that an undisclosed adjoining part was *rail* – so their drawings are no good.

Apologise for cheating and tell them that they should draw a road that cars go on. Again, inspect the drawings. Unfortunately, this time the word road came alongside an adjective, *closed*. What conclusions might we/they draw (haha!) from this exercise?

What is the difference in meaning between *man kills dog* and *dog kills man*? How is this difference created? Now we are beginning to look at the notion of sequencing and structure. Human language is the only sophisticated, structured language system in the animal kingdom.

By putting one word next to another, we are altering the state of the word. We are changing its meaning. The flexibility of words, their relationship with other words and the patterning of language for effect is the basis of grammar study.

3. The functions to which we put language

Pose the questions, "Why do we speak? Why do we write?"

The answer will typically come back that we speak/write to communicate. This is true. However, often people make use of language in different ways, ways in which no real sense of communication is made.

In David Crystal's *Cambridge Encyclopaedia of the English Language* you will find a proposal of eight ways that humans make use of language. This can be a really useful tool with which to introduce your course.

However, for me, the key is how you make use of this information. You could read the information together from the book. To my mind, if you were to do that, you would miss a wonderful opportunity to bring your course to life and to get the pupils thinking about the uses of languages straightaway.

In my experience, reading from language textbooks tends to lend the information that you are considering a certain permanence and 'correctness' that does not allow the pupil to form their own ideas, or indeed to work through those ideas. Things in books are 'right' and knowable. They are not really open to challenge. You read them, write them down and file them. I am not sure that the student will build a close enough relationship with the ideas from that approach. Also, you supplant the expertise in the room from yourself to the textbook. You have perhaps four hours a week of tuition time in the classroom. The pupils can read and write for you outside the classroom. It would be so much better for the pupils to be directed to read the Crystal material as follow-up work after you have discussed the ideas that **you** present in the form of a discussion session lead by you.

The functions according to Crystal in brief are as follows:

1   *To communicate facts and opinions*: the obvious answer to the question posed above. You will go on to outline seven other ways in which language is employed without 'communication' taking place.
2   *To express emotions*: there are occasions when people are merely using language as an outlet for their feelings. Imagine a person travelling alone through the Lake District.

They drive over the crest of a hill and a stunning view comes into sight. That person might utter, "Wow!" No communication is made here (there is no one else present with which to communicate!). In your classroom, you could roleplay this situation, or any similar scenario, questioning how language is being used.

3   *To support social interaction*: we use language to signal that we are comfortable in the presence of others or to establish a comfortable atmosphere. On entering a train carriage or taking a seat on a park bench, it is expected that we should say a few 'empty' words to the stranger present. Expressions such as, "It's a lovely day" or "Is this seat taken?" or "Morning" do not communicate anything. Their function is to create that acceptable atmosphere. This can be acted through by the group. Set up the train carriage scenario. Have a person enter a carriage in which there is one person already present. There is the vexed problem of where the new person should sit. Again, talk it through. Try the different seats. Examine the requirements of 'personal space' in a public place. Have the new person enter the carriage without saying anything. Let the silence linger a little. How does it feel? What will the effect of words be? What should our new person say? What is acceptable as a starting point for a conversation like this? Why would we begin a conversation with someone that we have no intention of ever speaking to again? As a group develop your thinking about the parameters of this situation. (Remember, you could have read this function of language out of a book! I think you will agree that now you have brought the whole idea to life and it has been an idea that could be thought about, reflected upon, evaluated, extended to other scenarios. Better than being read from a book and 'known')!

4   *For the sheer enjoyment of making sound*: sometimes we use our voices for the pleasure that can be gained from noises that we make. Why do people sing in the shower? What is to be gained from riddles and rhymes? Why is farting so funny? The possibilities for class work here are endless. Get pupils to make sound effect noises, to put on accents, to tell you what their favourite words to say are, etc., etc., etc. …

5   *To record facts*: clearly this is a primary function of writing. Sometimes we record things not for today or tomorrow but for years hence. Legal findings would be a good example of this. Statements of what happened in a court case have a general purpose of outlining principles. The names of the people involved will not be as important as the underlying ideas about crime and punishment that might be referred to years later.

6   *To give life a sense of shape, order and reality*: pose the question, "Why is today Thursday?" That is not an easy question to answer. Once you have got over the answer, "Because it was Wednesday yesterday!" you will need to investigate this. The answer is that we all agree that it is Thursday. Why do we all agree? Because we need shape and order to our lives. Language can provide these measurements and indicators. Another interesting scenario that you could set up to exemplify this idea is that of the wedding ceremony. Bride, groom and all guests turn up to hear a transaction of language that makes the marriage 'real'. Everyone leaves the wedding believing that the couple are now married. Language has created this reality. Clearly, there is fun to be had in setting up a marriage ceremony in your classroom!

7   *As an instrument of thought*: why do we talk ourselves through the assembly of flat pack furniture? Why do we revise for exams? Sometimes we use language to think with. This can lead to a broader discussion about whether it is possible to think without the use of language.

8 *To create our own identities*: your voice is a very important part of the way that you present yourself. Some of the features of your voice you cannot alter. However, some of the features of speech can be developed and honed. What things can you tell about a person that rings you on the telephone? The only indicator you have is the voice. Age, gender, ethnicity, regional background, educational level, mood? You could develop this discussion to consider stereotyping based on voice.

These, then, are the functions of language. They are a useful point for students when considering any text. If you consider the text in terms of its function it can support the understanding of how linguistic features, such as vocabulary choices, structures and voice, are being employed.

4. Taboo language

Here is an area of language use that is sure to engage the interest of your students. Gather your class round in a circle and create a continuum line in the middle. At one end you have *Acceptable*, at the other *Unacceptable*. Give each student a card with a swear word or taboo term on it. They then have a couple of minutes to think about their word by themselves. Then, in turn, each student introduces their word saying how they feel about that word and placing it on the continuum. The first person to go does not have any other words to measure where to place their word. They must make a choice based on how 'acceptable' they feel that their word is. Clearly, the task becomes more complex as the number of words put down increases. The discussion and disagreement will develop.

As your continuum fills up you can broaden the discussion. Are there any types of swear words emerging? Can they be grouped (bodily functions, sexual, moral stance, religious)? Why are the female sexual swear words thought to be more offensive than the male ones? Do you think that some swear words might be losing their 'strength'? Why might this be? Which of these words would you use in different situations? Why are the 'religious' swear words near the 'acceptable' end of the continuum? Would being in church change the strength of these words? Does the context in which the words are spoken have an impact?

A follow-on activity that can prove useful is to ask students to reflect on their own use of taboo language. This could be prepared as a piece of written work at home that forms the basis of a report back to the class. These reports would then form the starting point of the next lesson.

5. What's in a name?

We are only really familiar with one personal naming system: first name, possible middle name(s), family name. Around the world, there are all sorts of naming systems. Research into this could prove to be a useful homework assignment.

I make use of the fact that I have children and had a hand in naming them. Here are the details of the decision.

Table 1: Parental choice of names

Parents

First name	Middle name	Family name	Age at decision
Peter	Martin	Illingworth	28
Rachel		Ormsby-Ashworth	29

Children (twins!)

First name	Middle name	Family name	Age at decision
Adam	James	Illingworth	M
Laurie	Martin	Illingworth	M

Date of decision — 9 June 1994

Listed below are some potential reasons/factors that might affect how a person receives their name.

   Family names
   Names of idols/famous people
   Male line of surnames
   Fashion
   Gender
   Religion
   Race
   Nationality
   Patterns of sound
   Age of parents
   Fitting names with names of other siblings
   Personal events
   Place of living
   The seasons
   Names with a meaning
   Personal preferences
   Social class
   Physical appearance of the child
   Cultural values
   Whether to have a middle name
   The number of people making the choice
   Number of syllables
   Initials don't spell out some acronym
   Social pressures such as fear of bullying

This is not an exhaustive list but it should do for your group to get the point that naming, or labelling, is not a simple process.

   A good approach is to ask students to consider all the factors that come into play when the decision to name a child is made. I think that the record number that one of my groups has come up with is 22! A particularly enjoyable homework here is to get the students to name a child of their own, using their own last name (or last name of their girl/boyfriend!). Then, next lesson, each student feeds back, justifying their choices with reference to the factors outlined in the previous lesson.

Another activity that you could try involves photocopying the sections in the Yellow Pages for men's and women's fashions. The variation in the names of the various shops is surprising. Students could select the three shops that they would visit and the three that they would not. Clearly, the only thing that they have to base this decision upon is the name. An extension activity here might to be to design an advertisement for one of the shops based on the idea that they get of the shop based on its name.

I would suggest that you have material here, if you follow the sequence through, for a strong opening series of lessons. You have covered a great deal of ground, opened up lots of lines of enquiry and have not once referred to a textbook! As a group you have collaborated in discussing linguistic areas of interest. It is clear that you will be expecting everyone to 'chip in' to the work of the group. Individually, students have had lots of opportunities to think through for themselves and then to research ideas. Hopefully, you have managed to engage your group. Importantly, whilst allowing the students to come up with the 'knowledge' themselves most of the time, you will have presented yourself as the expert in the room!

Chapter 2

Audience, purpose and context

If you choose to base your teaching around the idea of investigating texts rather than using a textbook approach, you will need to give your students the critical tools with which to investigate. We will shortly consider the linguistic methods/frameworks that are used at A level. These methods are only really useful if you first approach the determiners of language transaction: *audience*, *purpose* and *context*. Students need to be able to locate the text as a genuine communication.

- Who is the audience?
- Why is the writer or speaker making the communication?
- What is the situation giving rise to the text?

Whenever anyone sets out to communicate using language there will be a *purpose* in mind. Sometimes this purpose will be clear. To write a note to the milkman saying, 'One extra pint today please' is fairly straightforward. This message does however also rely entirely upon the *context*, its situation. The audience is specific (the milkman), the vocabulary makes use of a contextually-bound use of the word 'pint', and the word 'today', whilst being written the night before, relies on the milkman finding the note the following morning. This communication, whilst being simple, relies on having the right context to make that communication successful.

Essential to our study of language is the idea that a text, whether written or spoken, has an *audience*. This audience, or very often audiences, will interpret the text, bringing their own sets of prior understandings, perspectives and viewpoints to bear upon the intended meaning of the writer or speaker. Effective communication must anticipate the needs of the audience, the commitment of the audience and the intended effect upon the audience.

It is very important that you drill into your students the understanding that the texts that you are considering together are not abstract pieces of language that serve no function other than to test them. The texts are real and have been plucked from real life situations. You can only really investigate a text if you are fully alert to what it is that you are considering. Time, place, author and purpose are important to an understanding of the language skills that have been employed. You cannot judge the effectiveness of a text in communicating if you do not consider to whom the text is appealing and the purpose(s) of the writer or speaker. Students sometimes struggle to appreciate the authenticity of a text. This can lead to some rather shallow and abstract observations about the nature of a text.

One way around this is really rather straightforward. You can encourage students to bring in texts that they find for themselves. Clearly these texts can come from any situation. If the student brings in a text they will appreciate the context from which they have taken that communication.

The following text is one that you might find in your filing cabinets!

Bloody Revolt

Geoffrey Chaucer and the Peasants' Revolt of 13 June 1381
One point that fascinates scholars about the life of Geoffrey Chaucer is his silence on the matter of the Peasants' Revolt. Chaucer lived in lodgings above the Aldgate in London, through which the peasants poured, intent on the murder of the officials of the Crown.

The peasants and disaffected Londoners were angry at the instigation of a 'Poll Tax' of three groats, to be paid by everyone whether they were rich or poor. They were also cross about attempts to fix the wage level paid to labourers. This revolt represented a break from the past and was, perhaps inevitably, violent and murderous.

Geoffrey Chaucer, as collector of customs (taxes), was exactly the sort of person that the peasants were intent on finding. They murdered many tax collectors and the palace of John of Gaunt, Chaucer's close friend, was burnt to the ground. The young king, Richard II, and his councillors retreated to the safety of the Tower of London. There is no record of Chaucer being there with them. If he were lying low in his lodgings at Aldgate, he would have been able to see the rebel encampment at Mile End as well as the strongholds of the city erupting into flames.

In the end, the young king addressed the rebels at a meeting in Smithfield and the Lord Mayor of London beheaded the leader of the rebellion, Wat Tyler. The king and his councillors had survived a great threat to their rule.

Chaucer was a wealthy man and an important man and certainly was in the employ and on the side of the king. In 'The Clerk's Tale' he describes the London crowd as follows,

> O stormy peple! Unsad and evere untrewe!
> Ay discreet and chaungynge as a vane!
> Delitynge evere in rumbul that is newe,
> Foe lyk the moone ay wexe ye and wane!

Chaucer did not have a high opinion of the people.

So why does Chaucer have nothing to say at all about what was a most momentous and important event in the life and history of the city in which he lived? He was definitely there. We know this as he sold his family house in Thames Street just six days after the revolt. We have the records of the deeds as proof.

Imagine that you are Chaucer living through the Peasants' Revolt. Describe the things that you have seen and the way that you are feeling. Perhaps in your writing you might draw out why you will not publicly write about the situation.

Presenting students with a text and asking them to examine it is a way of increasing their ability to analyse and, indeed, their sense of confidence in approaching unseen texts.

The above text about Chaucer is clearly from a genre that would be familiar to your students. It is probably a format that they take for granted. The starting point for analysis is that of defining potential audiences, purposes and genres. What is this text? What is the purpose of the communication? Who are the potential audiences of the text? From this opening, your students can then go on to explore how the text has been 'put together'. If they feel secure that they have identified the determiners of the text then they can begin to think about the language frameworks: namely grammar; lexical and semantic choices; phonological features; and discourse.

Students could look at the different voices in this text. There are three; the narrator of Chaucer's story, Chaucer himself and the voice in the task at the bottom. Is this a separate voice from that of the narrator? Is there a difference in the assertiveness of those two voices? What relationship is established within the text between reader and writer? Who holds the balance of power?

Students can bring in their own texts. They can lead sessions making use of their own resource. Approaching text analysis in this way encourages students to think independently about the text in front of them. It also encourages students to examine that text in front of them in isolation, examining it for what it is rather than as part of some set of abstract examples of language use from a textbook. I also feel that taking this investigative route to analysis encourages system. Method is learnt through practice. This approach will surely promote flexibility in considering texts. The skill of analysis learnt here will inform the approach to the whole of the course.

Audience, purpose and context need to be considered together if a full understanding of each is to be formulated. Consider the following transcript from the *Talksport* radio programme *Fisherman's Blues* hosted by Keith Arthur on Saturday and Sunday mornings between 6 and 8 am.

> Chip in Glasgow wants to know the best way to fish for Pike and what's the best lures to use (.) well (.) we could do probably a 12-hour show on the best ways to fish for Pike and the best lures for them (.) first of all you need to know where the Pike are and then the locations they are likely to be within that fishing and these may vary from (.) almost day to day (.) often seasonal because Pike are gathered together to spawn um and the smaller male Pike will be in the company of the female Pike that can happen any time from late February through to about the middle of May (.) you'll get the times they want to be in the deeper water (.) don't forget that we're almost at the southern limit (.) Pike don't go much further south (.) when they're called Northern Pike in America they don't go much further south uh than us so they don't like hot weather very much they're not that good in hot weather so make sure you treat them very carefully if you catch them through the summer months winter time is usually the best time to catch them they're usually more aggressive (.) as for the lures well there are as many lures as you can shake a stick at and it will vary from water to water (.) also how you want to catch them you can try many different ways of catching Pike (.) some people like to catch them on the surface using lures that displace quite a lot of water on the surface (.) even flies that can be used so as I say it's a very broad church the best thing you can do when you fancy fishing Pike is to take a look around see what successful anglers actually use ...
>
> *Key:* (.) indicates brief pause

With a radio programme, students need to consider who the *audience* is, past saying that anyone could be listening. This programme is on between 6 and 8 in the morning at the weekend. Presumably, the programme is aimed at the angler sitting on the riverbank, sea front etc. wanting company or background noise. If this is the idea of audience that the programme makers have in mind then it is to this audience they are pitching the programme. In what Keith Arthur says in this particular transcript there is a sense of a community (*the fisherman's community*) at large. This idea of community is very inclusive for those that understand the technical vocabulary being used and the references made but can exclude others, those who do not understand the 'language' of fishing. The very fact that there is a technical language being employed here is also a defining feature of the potential audience for the programme.

Students need to be taught that there is very rarely a single *purpose* to a language transaction. On the face of it, Keith Arthur is giving out information here that will help the listener appreciate the needs of fishing for Pike. He is speaking directly in response to an inquiry from Chip (a listener who has e-mailed in to the programme). However, his answer has a more general application here. Keith Arthur directs his answer to a more general 'you'. Clearly, given the sense of community that is being engendered here, part of the purpose of the show is to entertain.

Here we have a radio programme that is devoted to a specialist subject. Whilst the specialism necessarily means that a good deal of the population will not be interested, the show needs to appeal to as many people as possible. Radio programmes need to have audiences or they will not be aired. How does Keith Arthur manage to appeal to as many people as possible within the confines of the programme?

All of this thinking can be done independently by your students. Careful planning of the questions that you want to ask and the outcomes that you want to achieve, will mean that students can develop a full understanding of this way of deconstructing texts successfully.

Any communication between people in speech or in writing is all about audience, purpose and context. The struggling student can always be re-directed back to these key elements of language transaction.

Chapter 3

General frameworks

Grammar

The word *grammar* is one that most of your students will greet with a mixture of fear and loathing. They feel that they should know something about this area of language, particularly as they have put themselves forward for an advanced course in English language. Hiding their incompetence can then take up a lot of a student's energies. Armed only with the difference between a simile and a metaphor and a vague remembrance of a few other literary terms, students can actively dismiss this area of their understanding. (What's worse, you – the teacher – might be feeling this way too!).

> **There are words, then there are the structures we put them in**
> **– that is grammar.**

I think it is helpful to make grammar feel manageable by starting with this thought.

Language moves towards being sophisticated once two words are put together. Words need a context. Necessarily, the words are altered by being next to each other. Words need a relationship.

This is an easy starting point for discussing the ways in which we make language cohesive. Take any two words that have a relationship.

rail   **road**

Show the group one word first. Then, add the second word and have the students think through the way that each word is altered by the presence of the other.

It is also worth considering the skills of decoding that we have as readers. Offer your group the following text.

> yawynA I dekcuhc a tekcub fo retaw rednu eht lennek dna neht rehtona ylno ti t'ndid mees ot eb gnimoc tuo eht rehto edis. I thguoht ti saw kcum taht dah tliub pu ro gnihtemos os I tnew ni dna tog a eriw taoc regnah dna detrats gniparcs tuoba htaenrednu dna s'ereht gnihtemos ereht.

Ask the students to write down/consider the skills that they are using to make sense of this piece of writing.

We understand that we (not all cultures) read top to bottom and left to right. We punctuate words with spaces, and sentences with full stops. Once we understand that each word is written backwards, we apply the rule to reverse each word to all of the words. Then we notice that the words make sense in the order that they are in now and do not reverse the whole text.

A development of this discussion is to think through the idea that the meaning of words does not reside in the letters and words themselves. The meaning of words resides in the function(s) that we, collectively, put them to. For example, there isn't particularly anything table-like about the letters t-a-b-l-e in that formation. The letters are merely written representations of sounds. Indeed, the sounds themselves are merely representations. *The meaning is in the function.* This is a difficult concept for students to grasp but an equally useful way into investigating the way that we organise units of meaning.

The linguist Ludwig Wittgenstein offers an interesting sentence for your students to think about.

Colourless green ideas sleep furiously

This sentence is grammatically accurate. Adjectives, abstract noun, verb and adverb are all cohesive. Furthermore, when spoken aloud, the sentence sounds right. So what is it that means that this sentence makes no meaningful sense? We go back to that basic relationship between words that we put next to each other – they need a relationship. So whilst this sentence is cohesive, it is not coherent.

Word classes are another area of grammar that causes concern. A good starting point here might well be to concentrate on the way that words move between classes and it is the context and the use to which the speaker or writer has put the word that will determine the class.

Consider the three following words: fish, bridge, tie. On close inspection by your students it will become clear that it is not possible to say what class of word any of these words is in without context – *without the words that are next to the one you are examining.* This basic thought runs throughout the approach that I am promoting here.

The idea of studying grammar is one that comes with this almost instinctive resistance. We need to make it interesting and purposeful. In the same way that we might examine vocabulary choices for their effectiveness, we can consider the purposeful employment of grammatical structures. To be able to label and define the grammar of a text is little more than feature spotting. To be able to spot features and to extend that discussion to comment upon the effectiveness of those features will be awarded much greater credit by examiners.

Attitudes towards language production can often be usefully investigated in the area of grammar. Prescriptivists believe that one variety of the language has greater 'value' than other forms. Most obviously, this might be applied to the stereotyping of character traits to accents and dialects in Britain; Standard English, represented in dictionaries and formal situations being considered 'correct'.

Grammatical 'correctness' is another area of language production that arouses the ire of prescriptivists. Students will enjoy discussing the ways in which they are corrected by parents and teachers in their language production.

Some obvious grammatical changes are taking place at the moment. The prescriptivist despairs at the seeming current inability of the populous to make accurate use of the apostrophe. A closer inspection of the history of the comma would highlight the fact that the apostrophe has always caused confusion and rather uncertain usage.

Examine with your students the following examples taken from signs.

Everyone like's our chips

Browns Shoes

New potatoe's

Gent's Toilet

Wasnt/was'nt

Jones's/Jones'

One argument that will crop up is that the apostrophe does not really add much to our understanding. Who would not recognise the meaning of the word *wasn't* if the apostrophe was missing? The shop sign *Browns Shoes* has probably had the apostrophe omitted because it looks fussy – a prevailing thought about this punctuation mark. This lack of understanding of and, to a certain extent, lack of commitment to the apostrophe leads to its random deployment. You could certainly ask students to collect examples from real life. Students should also be encouraged to say how they feel about the impending loss of the apostrophe. Those thoughts could be collected and analysed.

The split infinitive is another grammatical issue that you could productively investigate. Traditional books of grammar will counsel against the placing of an adverb between the particle and the infinitive form of the verb. An example of this would be *to boldly go* or *to directly ask*.

In the nineteenth century there was a huge wave of hate for this practice. One very famous example is that of Sir Stafford Northcote's remark about the concessions he was prepared to allow in bargaining over a treaty with the United States in the 1860s. He said of the British government that '… in the wording of the treaty it (the government) would under no circumstances endure the insertion of an adverb between the preposition *to* … and the verb.'

George Bernard Shaw might not agree. Here is a letter of complaint written by Shaw to *The Chronicle* in 1892.

> If you do not immediately suppress the person who takes it upon himself to lay down the law almost every day in your columns on the subject of literary composition, I will give up *The Chronicle*. The man is a pedant, an ignoramus, an idiot and a self-advertising duffer … Your fatuous Specialist … is now beginning to rebuke 'second-rate' newspapers for using such phrases as 'to suddenly go' and 'suddenly to go' … Set him adrift and try an intelligent Newfoundland dog in his place.

One of the reasons that language is a fascinating subject to study is that languages are constantly changing. Indeed, when a language stops changing and adapting to suit the needs of its speakers, it will surely die. Change is one of the vital signs of a language. I can't tell you how your students will respond to the ways that grammar use is being manipulated. This is healthy because it means that you (and I) and your students are all learning together. Whilst your students look to you for wisdom and knowledge, it is also healthy for them to see you joining them in learning. How empowering for your students to think that *you* are a learner as well, in an area that we have already seen might be one that they feel weak in. Grammar is merely a set of structures that people choose to put their words into. The fact that it is susceptible to change should also be attractive to your students.

Together you can investigate not just the prestige that standard grammars receive but also, to add balance, the important functions that standard forms of a language can offer. English is increasingly a language that is used as an international form of communication. Standard grammatical structures, observed around the world in places where English is used, help with intelligibility. The notion of a standard arose in the 17th and 18th centuries when the language exploded because of trade and the strength of the Empire. There was a need to quantify the language with dictionaries and books of grammar. A by-product of this stocktaking was the idea of correctness in language. Students might well enjoy investigating the belief that there is a right way to speak and write. You might expect a reaction against this idea from young people but their stance is not always so clear cut.

Particularly early on in your course, there are many advantages to making grammar, as a framework, the matter of debate and opinion. It allows your students to think through how they feel about structure in language without feeling the weight of ignorance upon them. In practical terms, they need to be able to highlight the impact that a grammatical structure has on unseen texts, both at AS and A2 levels. Learning about grammar must not be a process of being tested on the comprehension of technical skills. That is a surefire way to kill off interest before it has had a chance to develop.

The rest of this section gives you three ideas for furthering student interest in grammatical structure: collecting 'bad' signs; a class-based activity about the sequencing of letters and words; and finally a consideration of grammatical features of texts from different times. Enjoy the grammar!

Fun with signs

Here is a sign on a Gents toilet door. Quite why the floor is wet is, of course, open to conjecture – and one suspects a few jokes! However, sticking to language issues, we could first ask why the words *toilet door* and *locked* are in blue whilst the rest of the words on the sign are in black. Interestingly, it is the colour of the words that create the grammatical structure and the meaning of this text. The sign is indicating that the door is locked, presumably so that people don't bash into the door as they push against it. The signwriter is probably hoping to stop those of us who would start forcing the door. The blue words carry a separate message and the blue colour allows those words to be read in isolation. Will this sign work though? Are we likely to try the door anyway, knowing that signs don't always get taken down after they are no longer needed? Have the users of this toilet done something wrong that is implicit in the sign? Hopefully, you can see the areas of investigation here: grammar, lexical choices, voice, discourse.

Figure 1: Toilet door

Sometimes a sign means much to the people that write it but virtually nothing to anyone who doesn't have the benefit of the context. Students could try to collect signs that are ambiguous to the point of being totally obscure.

(The answer: this sign is in a school canteen! Presumably the dinner supervisors punish children with shrill noises!)

Figure 2: Whistle

Figure 3: Gents

To continue your discussion of grammar you could make use of the above sign. Look at the debate that is taking place on this sign. Which of the corrections was made first? Which of the corrections is right? Why do people feel the need to make such corrections? Does the sign need either of the corrections in terms of communicating its function?

This can lead you into the prescriptivist debate. Students will revel in telling you the ways in which they have their language production corrected by everyone from their parents, grandparents, teachers and friends. Perhaps the category of friends might be the least obvious of these groups. Friends can often be very critical and pick up upon idiolects that seem to stand outside sociolects.

Figure 4: Vending machine

Some defy analysis and just require you to stand back and admire!

Figure 5: Tennis

Again, a collected piece of text for investigation. Here we have a sign with an impressive header for a Grammar School. The sign has a border surrounding the text which gives the sign 'shape'. Big and bold upper and lower case lettering make the sign highly visible. The lexical choices are all one- or two-syllable words so the building blocks of communication are in place. Your students might like to investigate how the sign could be 'improved'. Clearly, grammar is causing a problem here. Or is it? Is the message of the sign accessible? What about the discourse mark at the centre of the text, the full stop? Encourage students to collect their own 'interesting' signs.

Letters and words as sequences activity

Your students will take language use and comprehension for granted until you train them to be alert to its subtleties and nuances. Here is a lesson idea in which you investigate the idea of letters and words as symbols containing abstract meaning.

1   Present the group with the letter 'T'. Discuss what the two lines you have written up 'mean'. How do we agree a 'meaning' for these lines? To what functions could we employ this 'meaning'?
2   Tell the group that the 'T' is the first part of a sequence. Discuss what they expect the next symbol to be. Will it be a letter? If not, what could it be?
3   Note the fact that your 'T' is a capital letter. What does this add to the understanding of the symbol?

4   Now add the letter 'h' to make the sequence 'Th'. Ask the students to say the sequence. Do they blend the letters to pronounce the θ from the phonemic alphabet. 'Th' is one of the 44 sounds that make up English.

5   Pose the question: is this going to be an English 'word'? What is a word? Why does this combination of letters offer the potential for an English word?

6   Add the letter 'e', creating 'The'. This is clearly a recognisable word in the English language. Indeed, it is the most used word in the English language. Will this be the end of the sequence? What does 'The' mean? Does 'The' mean anything very much in isolation? What sort of word is it? What is the function of the word? What is the relationship 'The' has with possible words placed around it?

7   Add to the sequence as follows: 'Theater'. This now offers lots of potential to discuss the 'meaning' of the word and, doubtlessly, the spelling. You could consider the notion of right and wrong spelling.

8   Add to the sequence as follows: 'Theater of war'. What does 'Theater' mean here? We clearly have the sense of battlefield here. How does the sense created here adapt the denotative value of the word?

9   Clearly words only function in contexts. What might be the context of this piece of writing? Who might be the writer? What purpose might they be putting the expression to?

This sequence of active questioning should help your students to keep developing the investigative approach. It should also alert them to the demands placed upon the receivers of communication and indicate the levels of sophisticated language knowledge that we all need.

The Scarlet Letter

Nathaniel Hawthorne completed writing *The Scarlet Letter* on 3 February 1850. He lived through a time when authorship as a profession was evolving. The reading of books for pleasure had expanded from an élite group of patrons to a large audience across many walks of life. Hawthorne hoped that he had written a 'bestseller' that would be popular with everyone.

However, monetary gain was not the only motivating factor in Hawthorne's writing *The Scarlet Letter*. He had read about the involvement of his own family in the settling of Salem, Massachusetts and, to Hawthorne's mind more embarrassingly, the witch trials of the 1690s. Hawthorne perhaps wished to atone for the way that his family had behaved.

When looking at the linguistic features of any text written in the past, you need to gauge the difference between the text in front of you and how you would expect the text to be today. In this way, you are able to measure the ways in which language use has developed from that point.

Hester Prynne has conceived a child out of wedlock, a sin in the Puritan society of Boston. Her punishment is to be exhibited in the marketplace for three hours. She has to wear an embroidered letter 'A' on her clothing from now on. The 'A' stands for adulterer. In this passage, Hester emerges from the prison to be taken to the marketplace to be exhibited. Hester is a strong woman and a sense of this strength is demonstrated here. Consider the following lines from *The Scarlet Letter*.

> And never had Hester Prynne appeared more lady-like, in the antique interpretation of the term, than as she issued from the prison. Those who had before known her, and had expected to behold her dimmed and obscured by a disastrous cloud, were astonished, and even startled, to perceive how her beauty shone out, and made a halo of her misfortune and ignominy in which she was enveloped. It may be true, that, to a sensitive observer, there was something exquisitely painful in it. Her attire, which, indeed, she had wrought for the occasion, in prison, and had modelled much after her own fancy, seemed to express the attitude of her spirit, the desperate recklessness of her mood, by its wild and picturesque peculiarity. But the point that drew all eyes, and, as it were, transfigured the wearer – so that both men and women, who had been familiarly acquainted with Hester Prynne, were now impressed as if they beheld her for the first time – was the SCARLET LETTER, so fantastically embroidered and illuminated upon her bosom. It had the effect of a spell, taking her out of the ordinary relations with humanity, and inclosing her in a sphere by herself.

In approaching the grammatical structure of this passage, pupils will undoubtedly observe that the sentences are long. They might also point to the large number of clauses within these sentences.

There are unfamiliar lexical choices here, both in terms of words that have fallen out of popular use and others whose meaning has altered.

The voice/narration may well seem 'formal' and perhaps some will spot the dramatic tone.

However, pupils must guard against sweeping statements about the nature of the way that English has changed. William Trevor's *The Story of Lucy Gault* was published in 2002. Your pupils, having identified features of language change in *The Scarlet Letter* might change their minds when looking at the following passage.

Again we have a presentation of a strong central female character who has suffered a life-changing event. Her parents have lost contact with her and she begins a somewhat resigned lifetime of waiting to be re-united with them.

> For her part, Lucy did not wonder much about the nature of exile, accepting, with time, what had come about, as she did her lameness and the features that were reflected in the looking-glass. Had Canon Crosbie raised with her the question of going out into the world, she would have replied that the nature and the tenets of her life had already been laid down before her. She waited, she would have said, and in doing so kept faith. Each room was dusted clean; each chair, each table, each ornament was as they were remembered. Her full summer vases, her bees, her footsteps on the stairs and on the landings, and crossing rooms and in the cobble yard and on the gravel, were what she offered. She was not lonely; sometimes she could hardly remember loneliness.

Here we see long sentences and some words that might be unfamiliar to your pupils. 'Looking-glass' appears dated and the 'lameness' being described here is that of a physical condition. This meaning may not be the first one that springs to mind with young people who have shifted the meaning of the word 'lame' in a new direction.

William Trevor is creating here an atmosphere of sadness and regret but with a character that shows spirit in facing her situation. Writers work with the language available to them and, in some cases, drive the language on with new innovations.

Lexis and semantics

Increasingly, these two frameworks are being spoken of, and indeed examined, together. We considered, in the Grammar section of this book, the ways in which meaning does not necessarily reside in the words (lexis) themselves but in the ways that we choose collectively to allow the words to function. At A level the task is to look at how writers and speakers create meanings. A part of this is their selection of vocabulary.

Whilst the potential for examining words and the ways in which meanings are created is limitless, here are four areas of study that you might explore.

Specific lexical fields

Looking closely at the nature of language in a specific lexical field can be illuminating. The example that I will use here is that of legal language.

In the courtroom there are a number of linguistic patterns that can be observed. There are many formal and ceremonial lexical choices made. These choices are part of the way in which the legal system impresses upon the people involved in the proceedings that this is a serious setting.

May it please the court   Your honour   ... the truth, the whole truth and nothing but the truth

One interesting set of technical words that is employed here is that of very familiar words that have a very particular meaning within the confines of the courtroom. The meanings of the words are bound by the context in which they are being used.

Action = a lawsuit   hand = signature   said = previously mentioned

On the other hand, the use of deliberately archaic language also gives the proceedings an air of gravitas. Modern versions of the bible retain archaic language to give the text a sense of authenticity.

Aforementioned   heretofore   thereby   witnesseth

A mixture of Latin and French borrowings is still in use. These words indicate the controlling force and the esteem with which these languages were once spoken and viewed in Britain.

Alias   alibi (both from Latin)   appeal   counsel crime (from French)

A technical language has grown up around the courts. Some matters call for very precise and well understood lexis.

Felony bail negligence injunction defendant

Sometimes there is need for looser terms to exist so that the court is able to be more flexible in the interpretation of what is happening or in the judgements that are made.

Alleged   objection without prejudice   nominal sum reasonable care

If you decide to send a student to the local court when it is in session they will not be allowed to make an audio recording of what is said but they would be able to make notes.

There are plenty of other areas of life that would provide specific lexical fields that could be investigated. The language of the church, or indeed a range of different denominations of church, would prove to be a useful resource. It is most important for the students to be able to deduce the purposes and reasons behind the employment of particular patterns of lexis. It is one thing to spot a feature but a much higher order skill to examine and identify the value of that feature.

Idioms

Idiomatic expression can be a real eye-opener for your students. A few simple introductory phrases should be able to set them off in collecting hundreds of such expressions. Idioms are phrases in which the denotative meaning of the words (as in the dictionary definition) has nothing to do with the connotative meaning (the function of the expression in its context) of the words.

Here are some examples.

1   *It is raining cats and dogs*
2   *She was left out in the cold because she was wet*
3   *They were at sixes and sevens*
4   *Hold the mirror up to nature* (this last one from Shakespeare).

These expressions indicate the level of wordplay in the English language. They might also be considered in the light of trying to learn English as a foreign language. How would you explain such language use to a non-speaker?

Beautiful words

The British Council conducted a poll in 2004 that asked those being surveyed (over 7,000 respondents who were learning English as a foreign language and 35,000 respondents to an overseas website poll) to indicate the most beautiful words in the English language.

The results for the top 30 are listed below.

1 mother   2 passion   3 smile   4 love   5 eternity   6 fantastic   7 destiny
8 freedom   9 liberty   10 tranquility   11 peace   12 blossom   13 sunshine
14 sweetheart   15 gorgeous   16 cherish   17 enthusiasm   18 hope   19 grace
20 rainbow   21 blue   22 sunflower   23 twinkle   24 serendipity   25 bliss
26 lullaby   27 sophisticated   28 renaissance   29 cute   30 cosy

Of course, we can examine further here what it is about a word that makes it 'beautiful'. There would appear to be a mix of sound and meaning.

Your students could write a text that includes as many of these words, in as high a density, as they can. Listen to the tonal qualities and patterns. What sort of subject matter is to be derived from making use of these words? Does this list suggest a lexical field?

Your students could nominate their own favourite words and examine the reasons for the choices. Collectively, you could make a *beautiful word wall* and see if it matched up with the top 30 list in any way.

Assessing the way context impacts upon the 'meaning' of words

Look at the following transcript of everyday conversation. Jane has just dumped her boyfriend, John. Whilst she is talking about this to her friend, Amanda, John appears, wanting to speak to Jane.

> JANE: So I said to him right(.) I said John you are **not** going out with **me** anymore
> AMANDA: What did he(.) oh (.) hello John (...) alright?
> JOHN: Not really (.) Jane can we talk please?
> JANE: Why would **we** talk? What would **we** talk about?
> JOHN: You know what (...) please
> AMANDA: Well (.) I'll leave you lovebirds to it
> *Key:* (.) indicates brief pause

This is a highly charged situation. We move from gossiping at the start of this transcript, through to deliberately deceptive language and onto hurtful and pleading tones. One interesting feature of the transcript is the way that each speaker seems to be directing their words to one person but is actually talking to the other. For example, when Amanda notices John approach she says hello to him but is really indicating to Jane that they need to change the topic of conversation. When John says that he is not feeling great, the impact of those words is surely for Jane. When he asks Jane if they can talk, he is really letting Amanda know that it is time for her to leave.

There are a number of interesting lexical choices being made here. You could have individuals or groups take charge of individual lexical items. They could discuss the 'meaning' of their word in that context.

Right – this lexical item is being used as a discourse marker. It is part of building up the tension of the reported speech that is being related. It indicates that the listener should be paying attention (an ongoing check) and also indicates that the information coming up is going to be interesting.

Alright? – interesting to note here the various ways that this word is being employed. It is being used by Amanda to 'buy' time for Jane to compose herself for the difficult conversation coming up with John. It is also clearly an inappropriate question given that Amanda must know that John is not feeling alright. She may have used it because it is the sort of thing that we routinely say as an opening to a conversation or she may have chosen to say alright on purpose to heighten the discomfort of the situation for John or, potentially, for both John and Jane.

We – the emboldening indicates the emphasis being placed by Jane upon this lexical choice. She is recasting the lexical item from John's previous utterance. She repackages it for him suggesting that there is no 'we'. Here she is using it to suggest that their relationship is over. John had used this lexical item in a much more open and neutral way.

Lovebirds – normally means two people that are in love and very happy with each other. Here, given the context, the word seems to have a more negative or spiteful application. The application of this lexical choice to Jane and John appears to heighten the awkwardness of the situation. Perhaps too, Amanda is indicating that she is not happy to be shoo-ed away.

Please – ordinarily a very neutral word in its application. It is a learnt social nicety. However, here it takes on an imploring nature. The suggestion is that John has something very important, and private, to say. He might also be suggesting that Jane is not acting in the way that she should. There is some discussion about how this word should be voiced. A good deal of the meaning will be carried through how the speaker utters the expression.

Pragmatics

Pre-teaching thinking

This is the area of work, within the frameworks, that students often find hardest to grasp. In the more structural elements of language usage, it is true to say that there are only so many sounds, words and grammatical constructions that are in use. However, once you move into the domains in which language is employed there are endless varieties and determining factors to be considered: social niceties, unwritten rules and implicit understandings that shape the choices that people make when they speak or write.

The expression in everyday life 'to be pragmatic' means that a person makes choices based on their situation; one cuts one's cloth according to one's means. This is a helpful way of looking at the framework of pragmatics. What are the factors, in any given situation, that influence the choices of language made by a speaker or writer? What social and linguistic restrictions are placed upon people in different contexts?

Take the following situation: two colleagues greet each other at the start of the day as they pass each other in the corridor. They both say 'good morning' to each other. If they were to meet each other going the other way two minutes later, they would not say 'good morning' to each other again. Why not? What prevents this? What if you were five minutes late to work and the boss said to you 'good morning'? Could there be an implicit reference to your lateness? Would the boss have to be careful not to say 'good morning' in this instance if he/ she did not want to cause offence/worry? If one of our colleagues was on the way out that evening and they passed the other, they might say 'good night'. If that colleague went back into the office to collect something they had forgotten they might say 'good night' again quite comfortably. What makes the leave-taking acceptable in multiples but a greeting singular? Good question.

More good questions; if you are at someone's house and you need to visit the toilet, what should you call it? What are the factors that might determine your choice? If you were going to open a ladies designer clothes shop, what factors govern the choice of name that you give your shop?

Investigating influencing factors

Languages exist in time and space. By this I mean that at different times and in different places a language is being shaped by different people. Those people have different environments and contemporary lives to describe. That is why the English language has so many different variants in its usage across the world. A single communicable language can have different aspects of grammar, vocabulary and sound because of *time* and *space*.

Within a single and stable community, languages still move forward over **time**. An often quoted example of this comes from the mid-15th century.

> 'I have sent you diverse messages and writings, and I had never answer again'
> *from a letter written by Dorothy Plumpton to her father*

I have modernised the spelling but I am sure that you would agree that all the words individually are understandable. The general sense that she has written to her father often but has not received any replies is also here. Perhaps your students could investigate what has changed over time here if not the words themselves. Let's examine the sub-clause at the end of this sentence. 'I had never' would surely now be 'I never had', 'and' might be 'but' and 'again' might be 'any' and move forward in the construction, making 'but I never had any reply'. With the new version you could go on to see if that can be improved. The words 'never' and 'had' do not quite seem comfortable. In the main clause, 'diverse messages' and 'writings' seem outdated. What would your students suggest as a more appropriate modern voice? Does the apparent formality of the voice suggest something about relationships at that time?

Geography and, in particular, distance is also important (*space*). A South African desk dictionary will have as many as 20,000 words that are not immediately recognisable to a British English speaker. It might make a good starting point for the discussion of influencing factors to collect unfamiliar 'English' words from around the globe. Here you have an interesting way into opening a discussion about what exactly English is. What are the parameters of a language? When is a language a language and not a dialect?

Situations

The study of pragmatics is a means of looking at how language works past the literal meanings of words. As speakers of language we have some shared understandings about the context of language communications. Here are a couple of examples from everyday life.

CAUTION LAMBS
(a sign by the roadside on the Chatsworth Estate in Derbyshire)

This sign does not mean that if you see any lambs that you should tell them off or read them their rights! This is not some new species of killer lambs! The word 'caution' applies to the way that you drive and the word 'lambs', on this occasion, suggests that they might react unpredictably to cars passing along the road and that you might expect there to be some lambs in the vicinity. Context is the binding factor here. The sign only creates meaning in the context in which it is situated.

NCT Baby Sale – 2pm
(sign advertising a tabletop sale)

We are all perfectly well aware that there will not be any babies for sale when reading this sign. This is interesting because the words rather suggest that there will! There are further shared understandings in this sign. The use of '2pm' indicates that the sale will take place today and the use of the abbreviation 'NCT' indicates that you would know who the NCT are or that it does not matter whether or not you recognise this shortening.

As usual, we would suggest that your students collect examples of this kind of language use. It is, of course, absolutely everywhere around them. Having to look for and collect their own examples of context-bound communication will support their understanding of the more general principle that you wish your students to grasp.

Further areas of interest

We listed earlier in the book the functions of language. One of those functions is to create a reality. If we invest *belief* and *authority* in a speaker and context, then the words that they say can create a new set of psychological or social conditions.

- In a court of law the magistrates may decide that a person is guilty of a crime. There is then a general acceptance of that person's guilt and the prosecuted person may well be viewed in a different light. Having been declared to be guilty the accused, whether they feel wrongly done by or not, accepts the necessity of paying the required punishment. In a case, such as a road accident, a magistrate reviews evidence of an incident that they did not experience for themselves. The magistrate listens to the accounts of others and then makes a judgement about what has happened. The importance of language cannot be overstated here.
- You go to the doctor feeling that there might be something wrong with your health. The doctor discusses your symptoms and gives you a general check-up. The doctor decides that all you really need is rest and that there isn't really much very wrong, you just lead a busy life and it has got on top of you a bit. For most people this sort of message would be very comforting. The doctor says that there is nothing wrong with you. Because of the doctor's notional expertise, this very short conversation and cursory examination would probably allay most people's fears. The words of the doctor can have a strong psychological impact.
- At your wedding ceremony the minister says that you are to be married. You and your partner confirm in words your intention to marry and then the minster indicates that you are married. All of your guests put immediate faith in this pronouncement. The act of ceremony creates a context in which the words take on a real sense of authority.

No doubt your students can find more situations in which words help to create realities. We mark out our lives with language markers:

- *teenager*: what does it mean to be a teenager?
- *twenty-first birthday*: what makes this birthday special?
- *first-time buyer*: what are the implications of this label?

The study of pragmatics has its detractors. Some feel that it lacks focus. Some feel that much of what there is to look at is covered by semantics. However, to highlight the framework of pragmatics encourages really deep learning. *The relationship between the speaker's and the receiver's context and the choices of language is the very essence of communication.* The student who can consider texts, in an examination situation, for what they are, rather than as exam pieces sent to test them, will prosper.

Time, space, situations, belief, authority and realities all take language analysis past the level of structural examination.

Discourse

At A level the investigation of discourse involves the consideration of how the parts make up the whole. Sometimes this will involve looking at graphological features, sometimes following the construction of a line of development within a text.

Here is an activity that I have tried on many occasions and one that your students could try. It involves recording someone telling a story or recounting an event. Allowing the students to collect their own data helps them take ownership of the material that they are analysing. It is also good preparation for collecting data in the coursework investigation. They will need to work out a set of conventions to show the grammatical structures of speech. This is probably best done once the data is collected. How could you show emphasis or stress of particular words? How do you indicate a pause in the flow? How do you indicate differing lengths of pauses. Again, do not tell them, let them work a system out. There isn't a 'right' way to transcribe so let the students take ownership of this. It allows them to believe in their collection of data as valid.

Once your students have transcribed their recordings, they can then investigate how the person that they have recorded has gone about relating their tale. Pulling the text apart will help them find the discourse features. Lots of questions can be considered; how does the speaker give contextual background? How much prior knowledge is assumed of the audience? What appears to be the purpose of the tale? Which of the functions of language are being employed (see the Introductory Sequence of Lessons for the eight functions).

Here is the transcript that I made. In this extract, Aldo Manino, a native New Yorker, tells about his experience of the day the Twin Towers fell in 2001.

September 11 2001 I remember I was (.) eh (.) I'd just started teaching (2) History in New York City public schools system (.) and eh (.) it was a busy day (.) it was Primary day Primary Election day where the Democratic Party was having their (.) eh whose gonna run for Council, Senate and so forth anyway (4) I remember (2) I remember the weather (.) it was really really beautiful (.) beautiful Spring day (.) I mean Fall day and I went into work (2) no problem about 8.30 the school was just down from my house (.) and (3) when I was at the school the secretary says Aldo did you hear that a plane crashed into the twin towers (.) I said oh what a shame (4) thinking a plane (.) you know (.) a little Cessna a little 3-seater 4-seaters propeller plane (.) then I started hearing the sirens (1) fire engines ambulances police whizzing by I'm thinking Jeesh (.) how big is this plane (.) walked out of the school could see smoke coming over from Manhattan (3) so I walked over a little bit and you could see one of the towers was on fire blazing on fire (1) ah (3) I immediately ran back inside the school went back to my parents' restaurant and as I was walking back to the restaurant (2) the second plane hit people just started going nuts (3) we (2) school closed parents came collected their children they went home (.) it was a big mess no one was allowed into Manhattan unless you were emergency or medical services (1) I was helping the cops direct traffic (.) I actually

went up and grabbed an NYPD tee shirt I had (4) put that on (2) cops all around (.) I was getting them coffee (2) water helping people (.) phones were dead but allowing people to use the phone (.) trying to get some sort of signal (.) I guess the one thing that stands in my mind most is just *the smoke* (.) and the sirens (.) it smoked for a good month and a half two months afterwards it was still that hot it was still smoking (3) *unbelievable* (3) I don't like talking much about it but it's sort of ingrained in my memory (.) in fact sometimes when I hear sirens I get a little shiver down my back (.) hearing a plane a little too low (.) but yeah (1) 9/11 that was it (3) horrible sad (6) and that was just my first day of teaching my first job as a teacher (.) that was a big lesson
Key: (.) indicates brief pause

The transcript makes use of lots of standard means of indicating features.

A pause in the utterances is demonstrated by a set of brackets. A pause for breath or short gap is indicated with (.), whilst longer pauses have the number of seconds that the pause lasted within the brackets. Noticeably above, there is a long gap as Aldo chooses the word 'unbelievable', which he then chooses to emphasise. There is also a longer gap after the word as he allows that word to sink in. Maybe he is aware of its strength, maybe he wants the word to resonate with the listener, or perhaps he is still contemplating that word himself before moving on. Exploring the distribution of pauses throughout the transcript can help to determine fluency of thought, passages that are constantly being arranged and re-arranged 'on the spot' and, sometimes, maybe pre-rehearsed.

Emphasis is indicated by italics and bold font. Exploring the pattern of emphasis in a text can be revealing in finding the structural design. However, here there is very little emphasis. Sometimes when people recount difficult events or events that they do not really want to relate, as here, the speaker can tell the story with very little in terms of sound changes. Aldo's story is told in a measured and calm tone without any real insistence or reliance upon emphasis.

In Aldo's choice of starting point there is an assumption that the listener knows about the date and the events that made world news on that day. He gives the listener the date of the event and then has to check with a filler 'eh' whilst he locates himself in the story. He gives you background as to what he was doing when he first heard about the planes hitting the towers. He does not tell you why the planes hit the towers or any other contextual detail about the event. This is where the speaker assumes that his listener has this detail already and he therefore de-selects from the story that he might have told. However, the fact that it is an election day for the Democratic Party is a detail that history has not remembered so well, so the speaker feels that this detail is relevant and he uses it to help set the scene, along with the detail about the fine weather. This initial setting of scene is of course a learnt discourse feature from literature. Notice also how Aldo's memory of real events and times, and his sense of storytelling blur for a moment. The weather as he remembers it felt like a spring day. He quickly changes it to a 'fall' day. The scene setting gives no indication of what is to come. It offers contrast to the rest of the story. The calm beginning heightens the effect of the end of the story. Aldo may well have chosen this beginning because of the assumption that his listener has prior knowledge of the event he is to describe. He needs to offer a different interpretation or angle if his story is to offer something new to his audience.

As the story begins to gain momentum, the cohesion of the utterances and the sequencing of events seem to also become confused. Aldo seems to have left the school and gone to his parents' restaurant and then he is back at school and the school is closing. This is typical of the relating of 'real' memories in traumatic situations. Also, the climax to the story is approaching and Aldo may well be trying to keep lots of information in his head ready to add to the story whilst telling the next detail. Sequencing the information on the spot is not easy and the lack of clarity in the middle is indicative of this. Notice also how, in the middle of the story, Aldo closes down the sub-plot of being at school, which he no longer needs.

'school closed parents came collected their children they went home'

Then, the confusion at the centre of the event begins. Aldo's grammatical structures become in places like the telegraphic talk of children acquiring language, strings of content words without the connectives.

'water helping people'

You could say that it was not a time for words but for actions. This sense is communicated in the tumble of language. The chaos is communicated here.

Aldo's story reaches the climax at the emphasised words of 'the smoke' and the sentiment of the story is perhaps encapsulated in the other emphasised word 'unbelievable'.

How's that for an interesting activity for your students? Collect a story, transcribe and analyse how the story is sequenced! Marvellous! Trained linguists? Oh yes!

Phonology and voice

This particular framework is an integral part of investigating all manner of texts. It is about the delivery of communication; specifically, how something is said or written.

In speech

One of the potential reasons for this area to be difficult for the students to appreciate is the way in which we tend to value writing over speech. Whilst speech is learnt naturally, writing is taught at school. It has rules and regulations. Writing is corrected and there is a very particular way of doing things. We learn about writing before we take any formal interest in how speech works and this tends to mean that we view the workings of speech from the perspective of written forms. Students must be encouraged to view speech separately from writing. Train your students, for instance, to speak and write about *utterances* rather than *sentences* when they discuss speech. Students must be discouraged from thinking that speech is haphazard or sloppy or lacking in any kind of structure. The grammar of speech is, of course, markedly different from that of written grammar. Have your students listen to any speech and ask them to identify how utterances are organised. Sentences and punctuation marks are replaced by a sophisticated series of pauses and stresses. At whole text level, paragraphs are replaced by the basic unit of conversation, turn-taking. The fact that we have learnt to do all these things without school tuition does mean that we tend to take them for granted.

Phonetics is the study of all possible sounds that humans can produce. Phonology is the study of how humans make selections from this range to create order and system within a particular language. Most variations of the English language make use of 44 sounds. (A full phonemic table can be found in the Child Language Acquisition section.) This is only a proportion of the 150 potential sounds that the vocal chords are able to produce.

Our interest, at A level, in voice tends to be twofold.

First, the delivery of speech can have a huge impact upon the meaning. The way that words are said can change their meanings immeasurably, so much so that the word 'yes', for example, can clearly mean 'no' if the speaker's voice indicates it through the sound. Pace, volume, pauses, hesitancy and fluency can all indicate a number of things about the speaker. The confidence, or otherwise, of a speaker may come through. The mood of the speaker may be highlighted and this would certainly impact upon the communication transmitted.

Secondly, past the technical detail of how voices are employed, we can investigate the social impact that voices can have. People manipulate their voice to suit the situation that they find themselves in. Sometimes we move or alter our voices to be more like that of the person we are speaking to. This is known as convergence. We do this when we wish to express, or feel, a warmth or respect for the person. This convergence can be done knowingly, but is often a sub-conscious manoeuvre. Conversely, divergence occurs when we distance the way that we speak to a person, or indeed, with a group of people. This divergence indicates formality or, sometimes, dislike.

It becomes clear then that as individual speakers we all have a range of voices. Students need to appreciate that they don't just speak in one way and that they select the voice that they will use to suit the situation in which they find themselves. Students could collect examples of a single speaker in different situations, formal and informal perhaps, and note the ways in which they modify their speech patterns. This might include pace, emphasis, volume etc. It would also be interesting to look at the ways societal hierarchies impinge on speakers' contributions to a conversation; for example, do the young defer to the old?

VARIATION IN SPEECH

- *Pitch*: we can speak at a high level or a low level, or move between the two. A rise in pitch may indicate agitation or excitement.
- *Speed*: again, move between speeds for effect or because of necessity. Perhaps a speaker feels that they are about to be interrupted and they are keen to make their point before allowing the listener to become the speaker.
- *Volume*: what is indicated about a person's meaning when they increase or decrease their loudness or quietness?
- *Rhythm*: languages have natural patterns. Sometimes, as speakers, we move outside these natural patterns. Silence is an interesting area to consider here. The active employment of periods of silence within passages of speech can be used for a number of intended effects, and also can be an unintentional feature.

The features listed above are known as *prosodic features* of language.

Paralinguistic features

Some means of communicating, whilst in conversation, involve the use of noises and movements that help to craft meaning. This kind of communication is at the very 'edges' of language.

A good example here would be whistling. Ask your students what can be communicated with a whistle, how the communication can be enhanced by such a noise. Example responses might include the 'wolf whistle' to express attractiveness, a whistle to express how expensive or surprising or shocking a statement appears, or a whistle to add a musical tone to what is being said.

It is also possible to weep or laugh whilst speaking and this moderation of voice clearly adds strength of meaning to what is being said. The effects are normally immediately evident. We might also choose to change our delivery. What is the impact of whispering? The conversation can become conspiratorial. Often if one person begins to whisper, the listener will also begin to whisper when they respond.

Eye contact is another area that comes into play here. Research suggests that we look at a person and away from a person in equal proportion when holding everyday conversations. To look at a person for extended periods can be uncomfortable for the listener. Have your students consider when they might choose to hold the gaze of their speaking partner. We tend to do this when we are saying something particularly important or if we are indicating that we are bringing our turn to speak to a close.

An individual's *speed* of communication can be gauged by means of taking a recording of a fluent stretch of their speech and counting the syllables that they use over a certain time-period. In the English language, the average speed of speech is 300 syllables a minute. If you make recordings from, for example, the reading of the news on television and radio, you will find that certain types of speech move at different rates. News reading tends to move at a much slower rate, perhaps more like 200 words per minute. Your students could each take responsibility for collecting spoken data from differing settings.

In writing

Whilst writing is expressed in written rather than spoken grammatical form, the voice employed remains an important part of the impact that a text can have. Many written texts clearly 'borrow' from the language of speech in creating a direct appeal to their audiences. Again, there is an opportunity here for your students to collect such texts. Together you could develop a display of texts that share this feature in common. Having made your resource, collectively you can investigate why (*purpose*) written texts might employ spoken voices and the impacts that the writers hope to have (upon their *audiences*).

Give your students this opening stem to a sentence:

'Are you looking for ...'

Ask them to complete the text, advertising a product or service. Having researched the features of speech that written texts employ, ask your students to use as many of them as effectively as they can. Explaining their language choices to the rest of the group afterwards would be a healthy activity for a linguist to do!

Each time students investigate a text, they need to have that toolkit in mind: grammar, lexis, semantics, phonology etc. Phonology is an important part of the communicator's skill and is always worth looking at in both speech and writing.

Here is one final activity to try in this section.

The following is an extract from *Farewell but not Goodbye*, the autobiography of Bobby Robson, the football manager. Here he is talking about playing for England against Scotland at Wembley Stadium in 1961.

I was playing in newish boots and by the end of the match I had a whopping blister on the big toe of my right foot. Squeezing my shoe on after the game was eye-wateringly painful and I still had the journey back to the Midlands ahead of me – not in an FA limo, mark you, but by train and bus. Later, fleets of plush cars would wait for the players beneath the Twin Towers, and fan out across the country to deliver their precious cargo back to their families. For us, in 1961, it was off to the train station. You had to produce your ticket and any other documentary evidence to get your expenses from the FA. Walter would dish out the money and record every item of expenditure on an expense sheet. Taxis were discouraged as far too extravagant.

Before you read how I might suggest what this text could be used for, read it through and see what strikes you. This autobiography was published in 2005. The extract above details an event and time 44 years previous.

As with any text that you are investigating in any portion/module of the course, consider the base linguistic frameworks; grammar, lexical/semantic issues, voice and discourse. Select from that list. Which do you think would be most interesting in analysing this text?

Personally, I would choose *voice*/register.

Consider with your group the nature of autobiography as a genre. What is/are the purpose(s) of the form? Autobiography is about telling the reader what happened but must also be about, or at least involve, creating an identity through which those events are perceived. In this extract we are told about the difference between the pampered lives of today's top footballers and the rather more 'ordinary' treatment of players in an earlier era. However, we also get a sense of Robson's perspective on this difference. His language choices create a sense of identity. There is certainly a voice of experience here, but one of conversational fireside chat; the voice of fond reminiscence. Robson does not seem to feel the need to prove himself or to be impressive. His register here is familiar and friendly.

Having gained with your group a general sense of what the voice appears to be, you can then proceed to ask them to think through how the language choices and structures have been employed to create this voice.

Note: what about the use of the term 'Twin Towers' in 2005? A certain semantic shift has occurred. If none of your students pick up on this, make sure to drop it into the discussion. We can't know whether this is a conscious referencing of 9/11 ('precious cargo') or wholly unintentional. We can, however, discuss it!

Graphological features

Pre-teaching thinking

A note of caution

This is the poisoned chalice of the course. Students always want to write at great length about presentation. I think that this is because they perceive it to be 'easy' and also important to all texts in our increasingly showy, over hyped and flashy modern world. Whilst in some cases there can be a heavy reliance upon style to achieve impact in texts, this perception can lead students to over-emphasise the importance of graphological features, often meaning that graphology is written about first in essays and at great length, but often at a rather shallow level. Remarks like 'the background is green because this is an advert for Fairtrade coffee' whilst being a feature spotted, stops short of explaining why that might be relevant.

It is also the sort of observation that you might hope for at GCSE. I think that your task is to steer your students towards contemplating choices made by writers, editors, designers and publishers in the ways that texts are presented. Students need to be trained to say something useful about graphological features and to be selective about when to say anything at all about the subject. Sometimes the presentation is not a key framework.

Range and design options in the 21st century

Before the advent of the printing process the production of writing was an art form. Writing was produced by a skilled class of artisan. Texts were produced by hand, one at a time. The books were often extraordinarily beautiful, the product of many days of hard work. You could liken the work of the scribe to the work of the carpenter.

Whilst printing increased access to literature, one of the side effects was to kill off the artistic nature of text production. Perhaps the technological development of printing has returned the craft of presenting texts. This time, however, the artisans are all of us! Software packages, in-built laptop design features, endless font options etc. give us all the chance to present aesthetically pleasing texts.

I think that the best way to have students contemplate the relationship between presentation and content is to give your students a small design activity to do. One example might be to design a business card for a tattoo studio. Ask students to think through what information should be on the card. Make sure that every student is going to use the same content information, then send them to design the card. It might be a good idea to have some people work in a pair. This will add the layer of negotiation to the design process. This could be a feature of the ensuing discussion about design; how is the process affected if you are working with another person to produce a text?

Tattoo design may well have a set of pre-conceptions from your students. When they 'show and tell' the discussion will gravitate, and if not then you can push it, towards the relationship between content, context and design. With tattoo design perhaps your students will loosely identify a style, or genre, requirement that helps to define the limitations of what is required. A good extension of this idea would be to try to produce a really bad design for a tattoo studio business card.

In this way you can demonstrate that graphological choices are guided by certain variables: context, audience, purpose, technological limitations/options, finance etc. Once students have made one design you could get them to make a second from a different 'genre'. How about designing a wedding invitation? Here is a text that is often replicated and with a very clear set of variables. How will your students fit into the limitations of the style but make a design that will please the happy couple?

Having made use of the design options open to them, your students may well be better equipped to examine with greater analytical adeptness the efforts of printed texts. You could extend the activity above by then bringing in a range of pre-existing tattoo studio business cards and wedding invitations.

It is the link between design choices and their intended effects that needs to be made by your students so that they can comment effectively about this in exams.

Impact on the challenge of reading

Here is an example of how the act of reading has changed and developed in the age of the information super highway. Older generations often berate the young for not reading enough or for not being able to concentrate on reading. However, I do not think that older generations ever had to deal with the level of complexity that is offered on the internet.

Technology is placing new demands on the young; reading, in truth, has changed immeasurably. Figure 6 is packed with interlinked information, but where do you start? Would all people start in the same place? Do we still start reading a page at the top and to the left? Has the new presentation of text meant that the centre of the page is now the starting point? Is there any start or end point to this page? Will different types of readers search this information in different ways? Does the text or texts on the page work in new ways structurally? How would a casual browser approach reading the page? What impact does this kind of presentation have upon the idea of concentrating on text? Does the fact that people spend a good deal of time accessing information through this medium impact upon the use of more traditional reading media?

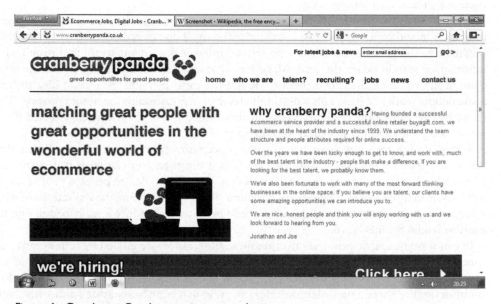

Figure 6: Cranberry Panda recruitment webpages

The whole idea of webpages borrows from the book form. However, movement between 'pages' is not linear as it would previously have been. Again, speed of access and movement is the key to the new structure of webpages. From this homescreen there are many ways of moving on to a new screen. Clicking on various links all over the page sends the reader in different directions through the pages. The links are endless.

Colour here is being used to accentuate the different topics and links. Images, fonts and size all compete to draw the eye to different areas on the page. An interesting development in terms of this discourse and layout is the way that lots of unrelated content is crowded onto the same page. This adds another reading skill: sifting through material to find the information that you are specifically interested in.

The screen illustration link referred to below is for the homepage of the town of Diksmuide in Belgium. Another way to assess the significant graphological features of a text is to isolate that variable. The website is in the language of Flemish. If you remove the recognition of the language itself then your students can concentrate on the impact created by the graphological features.

www.diksmuide.be

Because this is a home page, it offers lots of opportunities for the reader to click on to further pages. There is an expectation that the reader will choose a link that is of interest depending upon their individual interest. The understanding is that the reader will not read all of the page. The different sizes and shapes of font mean that you are able to read just some of the text and move on effectively. A reader with low commitment to the text is encouraged to stay with the text because of this feature.

Link between purpose and graphological features

In the note of caution, I challenged the way that students sometimes handle the importance of graphological features. This is not to say that graphological choices are not in themselves often very important. The activity of creating a good and bad tattoo studio design card will indicate that graphological features are potentially going to be the defining success or failure of the impact that a text can have upon the intended audience. Maybe writers in the modern age consider design opportunities much more early in the creative process then they might have in the past.

In the field of advertising, the element of competition with other texts heightens the need for effective presentation. The range of potential locations for texts today is vast. You could investigate the impact that differing locations has upon design options. A promotional campaign for a product could include television adverts, magazine space, billboard posters, cold sell leaflets through doors etc. It would be useful for students to investigate how each of these locations would impact upon the presentational needs. When the purpose is to persuade, as with advertising, then the writer must consider the location of their text when making design choices so that the impact of that text is as great as is possible. A billboard in a train station will not be able to carry as much actual text as a flyer dropped through a door and will therefore have to rely more heavily upon visual impact to create an effect. An activity that can help your students to appreciate this contextual factor is to show them a range of texts and ask them to suggest where those texts have come from. In their guessing the locations you can investigate how they have come to their conclusions. What is it about the texts themselves that suggests their locations?

Looking at the links between the core frameworks at A level can only be healthy for students' overall ability to analyse the relationship between producer, receiver, purpose and context. Graphological concerns can often illuminate the interdependence of choices in grammar, vocabulary, structure and presentation in creating and relaying meaning.

Chapter 4

Conventions of written and spoken texts

Pre-teaching thinking

Many of the available specifications consider this area of study in some depth, sometimes explicitly. The distinctions between speech and writing also underpin this course.

There are a couple of issues you need to be aware of and around which it would be sensible to plan.

First, your students will probably undervalue the medium of speech as a communication tool. It is innate and students tend to take it for granted. This will probably be the first time in their educational experience that they have been asked to consider the mechanics of speech. Much of their schooling will have focused upon writing. Writing is an abstract and artificial representation of language. It tends to make up about 2% of our communications in contrast to the 98% of our communication being oral. Writing has inflated status within the educational system. You must therefore be sure that your students develop an appreciation of spoken communication and all its subtleties. Students must be encouraged to see it in different terms from standard written forms. Students often want to say that speech has 'no grammar' or that it is 'wrong'. When they say these things, what they are really identifying is that the grammatical structures of speech are different to those of writing. It is interesting then to note that they describe that difference in terms of being incorrect. This demonstrates the fact that written forms are held to be the 'standard'.

Secondly, modern forms of communication, such as email, social networking sites and the like, are increasingly blurring the lines between writing and speech. For example, with 'chatting' on a social networking site, the pen and paper of the written form are represented by the keyboard and screen of the computer. The sender is able to craft responses and to make changes before sending. However, the medium is fast and to maintain a 'conversation', the responses need to be made quickly. The advent of the webcam facility means that you are also able to see the person to whom you are 'speaking'. A whole new hybrid set of communication forms is developing and re-developing at a rapid rate. Elements of speech and writing are evident in all these new forms. Investigating these new forms is going to make up a significant part of your study in the language and technology section of the course. Whilst looking specifically at speech and writing it would perhaps only really be necessary to assure yourself that your students can identify and distinguish between those features of new technologies that are like speech and those that borrow from writing.

I think the most helpful approach to take would be to start with the language of everyday conversation. You could then make that your starting point, or perspective, from which to analyse other spoken forms, such as prepared speeches or sports commentaries.

Quantifying the differences in other spoken forms can most usefully be achieved from this starting point.

Factors that affect the manoeuvres of everyday speech

The basic unit of a conversation is *turn-taking*. You have a go, I have a go, and onwards. This is true of all languages. It is not always observed in the ways that we might be familiar with. There is one tribal island language, which shall remain nameless so your students could research it for themselves, in which all the men get to say what they want first then the women are allowed to speak afterwards! Not what we are used to, but turn-taking all the same.

However, turn-taking is not a simple process. A speaker does not simply stop talking and another speaker begins. There is a whole series of factors and signals involved in this highly sophisticated manoeuvring.

- *Status* plays a key role in the organisation of conversation. Age, power and gender can all be factors here. In situations where one speaker is deemed to be more 'important' than the rest then a number of features can normally be observed. Such conversations tend to be structured around a certain deference toward the important person. Participants are more likely to wait their turn rather than speak over each other.
- Some conversations have what is known as *pre-sequence*. This means that the participants share an understanding of what has been said before. The conversation is part of an ongoing sequence of conversations. This tends to lead to context-bound expressions being used ('you know what she was like yesterday') that indicate the closed nature of the conversation. A full understanding of what is being said by the participants can be difficult when analysing a transcript.
- *Adjacency pairs* are coupled expressions in which an opening expression is followed by a recognised response ('Alright?', 'Fine thanks, and you?', 'Fine.') Much of the use of adjacency pairs is in this light, ephemeral talk.
- *Intonation, volume and speed* can all act as indicators of the manoeuvres of conversation. As we come to the end of a turn in a conversation we tend to slow down and the tone of voice may well drop. If we can see that someone else is about to join in, or more controversially interrupt, we may speed up to complete what we wish to say.
- *Stereotyped tags and trailings away* often indicate that a turn has come to an end. ('We'll have to wait and see', 'Makes you think doesn't it').
- Conversations sometimes have what is known as a *general script or framework*. If you go to buy a train ticket from the booth at a train station, then both you and the attendant have a general understanding of your roles in the conversation and the shape that such a conversation should reasonably take.
- It is also observed that the *current speaker* has the right to be heard. To interrupt is often rude and can lead to the breakdown of the conditions for a conversation to be successful. This can be easily observed in television or radio debates. If the current speaker does not yield to the person that interrupts then both people try to speak over the other and communication is quickly lost.
- *Eye contact* is a relevant feature here. Ordinarily we look at and away from the person we are speaking to in equal measure. To look more fixedly at the person you are speaking to can have a major impact upon communication. We tend to do this if we are saying

something very important or if we wish to assess comprehension in our listener and also when we are ending a turn.

THE IMPRINT OF THE VOICE

The way that you speak carries a number of identifying marks that you will not always be able to disguise or alter. In assessing speech it is important to bear in mind the fact that the utterances are spoken and as such there is a lot of information carried past the vocabulary used. The way in which we speak is thought to be more important than the words that we actually say.

When you are speaking there are three factors that affect the impact that your utterances have. First, there is the utterance itself. Research indicates that only 17% of your message is carried by the words themselves. Secondly, the way that you use your voice to give out meaning carries 38% of the impact made. Finally, what you are doing at the time is thought to be most important, carrying 45% of the effect created. We often spend a lot of time planning what to say when we have an important discussion ahead of us. It would appear that this is time that is largely wasted.

THE WAY THAT YOU SPEAK

It is clear that your voice does some of the talking for you. People are listening more to the tonal qualities of your voice than they are to the words that you say. It is worth considering the things that people are listening to and thinking about the judgements that they are making based on that listening.

WHAT YOU ARE DOING AS YOU SPEAK

This is more commonly known as body language. This factor radically changes the context of the utterances and as such has a large bearing upon the impact that those words make. One excellent example of this is the handshake. Varying degrees of formality follow a strict code of usage.

The passage above ('The imprint of the voice'), can make a useful starting point for investigating the nature of speech. One activity that I have tried, that has gone down very well, is to ask students to prepare what they would say if they were going to ask someone to go out on a date with them. Once the feedback begins it will become evident that they have spent all their energies in 'writing' a script, choosing the words carefully. If you then introduce the points made above, it can provide the basis for a discussion about the value of spending all that time choosing the words.

Building a first transcript

One way that students can begin to investigate the grammar of speech is to collect a stretch of everyday conversation for themselves. Having recorded the conversation on a phone or dictaphone, students need to think about how they will divide the utterances up on the written page to show how the words are spoken. They will need to find a system that can indicate the pauses and how long the pauses are. They will need to indicate those words that have been emphasised more strongly. And how will they show simultaneous speech as the participants of the text speak over each other.

Students should, hopefully, notice that utterances do not fit neatly into written units like sentences. They will also be able to observe the umms and ers and filling sounds that can be employed for a range of reasons such as preserving a turn or creating thinking time. Sometimes, people change what they want to say halfway through a thought and sometimes they refine or alter utterances. In making your students develop a set of solutions to show these spoken features in a transcript, you will be helping them define the grammars of speech. If they can actively see that speech does not follow the rules and conventions of written forms then they will begin to see the differences. This is important in moving away from the idea that writing is intrinsically right and that speech is, in comparison, clumsy.

In using everyday conversation as a yardstick, your students can now be encouraged to investigate other forms of speech. Some prepared texts in more formal settings would create clear differences from everyday speech. The language of a sermon from a pulpit or the language of a politician's speech would noticeably lack many of the features of everyday speech. Indeed, such texts would move much closer to written expression. There are plenty of spoken forms that sit inbetween these extremes. An easily accessible stretch of speech that can be collected is that of stand-up comedy. Such a text will have a generally prepared nature but comedians often have to respond to an audience and also have to appear to be thinking on the spot. When texts have a spontaneous element within a general framework then there is much that can be identified by your students. Sports commentary is another good area for this sort of analysis.

The working wall

The walls of Sixth Form schools are often left bare or are covered with posters for Shakespeare plays. In my room, the walls are reserved for the work of the students. They are not really up there for formal neat display but because we can actively display, in this instance, the transcripts and other working documents. A student might mount their transcript onto a piece of A3 paper, making annotations around it. Then, as the student makes their presentation to the rest of the group, the transcript is placed on the wall and we gather round it. These materials can then be collected on the walls, making a visible record of the learning that is taking place.

A further good example of this is provided by the AQA Specification B AS examination. In the exam, students are presented with seven unseen texts that represent different varieties of language use which they then have to group together in terms of linguistic interest. In preparing for this exam, students can collect their own texts and create a resource from which to revise and to complete practice answers. The groupings can be displayed on the walls. Better still, the groupings can be taken down by other students to work with. This seems to me to be an excellent use of the walls in your room.

Speech is taken for granted and your challenge is to help your students appreciate its complexities and the ways in which it manoeuvres. Everyday speech can be contrasted with standard written forms – and with other types of speech production. Hybrid forms of language communication, such as internet social networking forums, can illuminate not just the differences between speech and writing but the increasingly blurred division that exists there.

Chapter 5

Language in society

Gender

Pre-teaching thinking

Understanding language in any given social context depends upon a student's abilities to see the relationships between their own life, language and society. These factors can be taught and understood as discrete areas, though considering the ways they interact in the process of making meanings is far more productive and should be regarded as the ultimate aim of the course. By doing this, students are learning that language and meanings do not just 'exist', but that language is living and human beings create and make it.

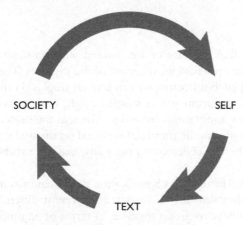

Figure 7: Society–self–text diagram

This diagram explains how *Society, Self* and *Text* are reliant on each other if meanings are to be fully understood. Alone, any one of these areas can be fascinating to examine and explain and during the course it is useful periodically to look at them in isolation. All work, however, should be constructed with the overview of working towards textual analysis that requires concurrent consideration of these three strands of meanings.

This part of the course is designed to allow you to create opportunities for students to learn about how society, self and text interact and to uncover the layers of meaning in any given text. Through reading and writing and the continuous study of linguistic frameworks your students will gain skills and confidence that allow them to assert their understandings of language and gender.

Society: This means the cultural and ideological influences on how meanings are made and changed. It demands awareness of historical shifts, political constructs and contemporary culture. It also includes understanding of our collective identities.

Self: This means how an individual's experiences, attitudes and beliefs affect the ways texts are read. It demands awareness of personality, individuality and how well we know ourselves. It also includes how each reader's unique identity informs understanding.

Text: This means any visual medium that can be read; it demands awareness that reading goes beyond written texts and should be taken to incorporate body language, images, symbols, juxtapositions and sites in which texts are found. It also represents the immediate object of study for students writing in examinations.

Gender-neutral language

Here is an area of interest that should encourage debate. The aim of gender-neutral language is to remove assumptions about the roles of gender groups. Those that advocate the removal of gender specific language would call this prescriptivist approach inclusive and non-sexist. Others might argue that it is a further example of the excesses of political correctness. As a forced or artificial change to language it is always going to create divisions in opinions. Students often feel that it is wholly unnecessary to worry about; until they consider the matter carefully.

1   Consider the following job terms.

Postman   Postwoman   Postperson   Postie

Which would you use if you knew that your post was delivered by a woman?

Actor/Actress   Sculptor/Sculptress   Poet/Poetess

What is the point of indicating gender in the above terms?

Female judge   Male model   Male nurse
Female referee

What is indicated here about the people in these particular professions?

2   UNESCO released a leaflet entitled Guidelines on Gender-neutral language in 1999. Over the previous decade the organisation had increased its resolve to tackle gender-specific language. The introduction to the leaflet muses:

'... language does not merely reflect the way that we think: it also shapes our thinking ...'.

This is a good starting point for discussing the idea that the English language is male-dominated and that women will not be able to claim equality in a culture that speaks in such a way.

Reading gender and reflective writing

This activity is designed to enable students to consciously and creatively engage with the three strands of language and social context. The texts are from gender-specific websites and offer advice and guidance on fashionable dressing. The first is aimed at women, the second at men.

Begin by gathering ideas from students about gender roles in the parts of society with which they engage in their lives. Record the ideas and they will become a valuable reference point during the course of this sequence of lessons. The discussion should be sustained for at least 20 minutes, though it can easily be sustained for an entire lesson. Sharing the time between independent talk between students and whole-class discussion will allow for a freer flow of ideas. Be explicit that you are considering *Self* and *Society* here.

Starting points can be offered, for example, explaining the roles that you adopt during your day acts as a model to follow. I explain that I am a male English teacher in a field where male teachers are less prevalent than female teachers and how this affects relationships in my department; that I am a son and a brother and in my family gender roles are at times quite distinct; that I a man with a female partner and how gender affects my relationship and how this is very different from the traditional gender roles fulfilled by my parents, now in their early sixties. Wider categories like school, sports, socialising (alcohol preferences are interesting here!), work or driving are other useful prompts.

Show the class both of the following texts. Explain their contexts, for example that readers would have either sought them directly or found them through a search engine; that they are small extracts from websites with many pages of advice; that the authors of these pieces are unknown; that they are accompanied by adverts and links to sites where one can spend money and they are probably read in isolation but website users belong to a form of community. Be explicit that you are now adding the study of *Text*.

Pose the following, or similar, questions, annotate texts and discuss:

1   How are women and men portrayed in these texts?
2   What assumptions do these texts make about women and men?
3   How do the writers use semantics and pragmatics in gendered ways?
4   What voice do the texts adopt?
5   How do the texts differ in the expectations they have of the ways women and men behave?

- Remember to finish off every outfit with the right accessories.
- A one-buttoned jacket and long trousers will instantly slim the body.
- If you have larger thighs go for boot cut trousers to make them appear slimmer.
- To create longer, leaner legs add a pair of high heels to your outfit.
- Avoid wearing trousers too high and too tight on the waist. Choose a heavier fabric in a larger size if necessary.
- Don't wear horizontal stripes if your aim is to look slimmer.
- Vertical lines and chevron will help slim down and flatter the torso.
- If you have got great legs don't be afraid to show them off in a skirt. If you are pear shaped 'A'-line skirts are much more flattering than pencil skirts.
- If you're too afraid to wear a lot of colour why not try adding a colourful scarf to a black ensemble?
- Every good outfit should have a good foundation so the right underwear is very important.
- Be careful of wearing white and pastel shades in less expensive fabrics as they are not very forgiving.
- Choose tops that overlap the tops of your trousers to avoid displaying unwanted bulges.
- Avoid high and polo necks if you are top-heavy. Stick to scoop and v-necks.
- A good hairstyle can finish off a look therefore it's important to have regular cuts with a reputable hairdresser.

Source: www.styledoctors.com/content/fashiontips.html

We all have that friend. You know, the guy who everyone else notices and who always looks perfectly put together. It's no lie; some people just have that flair – the ability to spot trends and even start some of their own.

Believe it or not, there's a trendsetter in you too – you just have to find him. Staying aware of the latest styles is not an innate thing, rather something that anyone can develop. So whether you want to always look stylish or be ahead of the style curve, your chance is right here. Come right in.

What exactly is a trendsetter anyway? He is the one who follows his personal style yet manages to pull off a look others find admirable. And even if others don't approve of his taste, he still wears what he likes. Whether or not he follows the norm, he looks great and inspires others to dress just like him.

It might seem like only fashion designers or those in the industry have the ability to spot trends early on. The trick is not to focus on how you can actually set trends – simply start off by knowing how to *identify* trends and take them to a whole other level.

Source: http://uk.askmen.com/fashion/trends/53_fashion_men.html

These texts are rich sources for discussion and exploration. Let us build some analysis using the linguistic frameworks that enable your students to build a full understanding of text, society and self.

Both offer semantic fields that capture the essence of the articles. In the 'Style Doctors' piece 'accessories', 'slim', 'longer', 'leaner', 'flatter', 'pear-shaped', 'outfit', 'fabrics' and 'hairstyle' is the beginnings of a list that relates the article quite generally to a semantic field of appearance. The language relays to the reader the importance of style choices that need to be made in order to successfully present oneself to the world. I use the word 'need' deliberately here; working alongside the semantic field is a sequence of grammatical structures which carries ideological implications that are discussed below. In general, the semantic field is one which demands that readers see themselves through the eyes of an inspecting audience. There are implications about judgements that will be made and emotional connotations tied to the visual impact of one's appearance. Get your students to explore their reactions to these things. Ask them to reflect on the judgements that they make about others' appearance, to consider their own style choices and to delve into ideas about how linguistics and body image are closely related.

Grammatically, the piece uses imperatives and declaratives to share its message with the reader. 'Every good outfit should have' and 'be careful of wearing white and pastel shades' are examples of declarative sentences which serve to instruct the reader. The confident tone and unarguable truth also creates a relationship of trust; the writers are obviously expert if they are able to state these 'facts' with such unambiguous clarity. As an aside, the name 'Style Doctors', with its appropriation of a title reserved for those educated to doctoral level, is a further attempt to enforce this view. Imperative sentence structures work in a slightly different way. 'Remember to finish off every outfit with the right accessories' can be anlaysed to exemplify this point – your student can do the rest. The imperative structure deems the content of the statement to be unquestionably good advice. Opening the sentence with the verb 'remember' shows the reader that it is simply a case of jogging one's thoughts about how to dress rather than being in possession of unattainable wisdom when making choices about style. The verb phrase 'finish off' adds to this effect; the writers indicate that detail is a key feature of style. Adjectival components of the noun phrases 'every outfit' and 'right accessories' are central to untying the grammatical complexities here too. 'Every' works alongside 'remember' to reinforce the idea that one must never lapse into dressing without careful thought over combinations of clothes. 'Right' works to compliment the reader's ability to demonstrate some judgement over what this choice might be. It also allows for seasonal changes and shifts in fashion. This adjective reappears later in relation to underwear. Encourage your students to explore the implications of these grammatical structures – once you have enabled them to see these features the next level of analysis is to relate them to the Society/Self/Text cycle. By doing this, they are successfully demonstrating the analytical skills needed to succeed in the study of language and social contexts.

Studying discourse means that your students can take the detailed analysis they have developed so far and see if their findings are supported by a consideration of the text as a whole. Does the overall impact of the text tie in with their judgements? Does the use of bullet points as a textual structure work alongside grammatical and semantic choices that have been made? Looking at the rest of the website, and possibly other texts in this field, ask – does the language of fashion and style carry implications about women's place in society?

Placing these readings alongside the study of the extract from askmen.com makes the entire process richer still. Analyse the semantic field that the writers have employed and compare its implications with the Style Doctors' piece. Ask students to explore the use of interrogatives and see if they think it affects the relationship between reader and writer. If so, what can they begin to deduce from this? Finally, ensure that your students investigate the differing nature of the tone of this discourse – its informality contrasts sharply with the first piece.

Finally, a word of caution. During this part of the course it is your students' responsibility to gain as full an understanding of the ways in which genders are represented linguistically in our world. They should not come to rash conclusions about sexism, body image, differences and similarities between men and women and writing for different genders based on a few short articles. It can be tempting for young scholars of linguistics to seek to reinforce views they maybe already hold; our task as their teachers is to enable them to look at every text and every linguistic phenomenon critically.

Then, to give the students an opportunity to reflect on the ideas that have been discussed set three questions, to be completed outside of the classroom. These questions provide some of the most engaging, revealing and thoughtful pieces of students' writing one ever gets to read.

1   How would you explain the ways gender affects your life?
2   What are your views on gender and society today?
3   With reference to any texts studied, how are different genders represented through English language?

Here are some extracts of responses to these questions from students in recent years.

1   **How would you explain the ways gender affects your life?**

'If I were to be put in a category, I would probably be more masculine than feminine'
'Being masculine or feminine largely depends on your actions.'
'I find myself defending women regularly.'
'The type of language I used isn't very "ladylike" in my opinion.'

2   **What are your views on gender and society today?**

'Why is it that if a female has a lot of partners she is seen as a slag or worse?'
'For instance, The Spice Girls' success was due to nothing more than their exaggerated sexuality.'
'I am completely open-minded and accepting of different people's feelings and attitudes to their gender, and I think if everyone else was comfortable and less narrow minded, it'd help to understand a lot more about the society we live in today.'

3   **With reference to any texts studied, how are different genders represented through English language?**

'I believe the reason women nowadays are much more conscious about the way they look [is] because of the media.'
'There is a distinct difference in the way that the two genders are represented within British society, which is full of stereotypes.'

Reading problems and writing Commentaries

Writing by and for people a little younger than Sixth Form students will provide examples close enough to students' experience for them to have some expertise in the subject and far enough removed for them to be objective in its analysis.

Problem pages from teenage girls' magazines are a good area for engaging and productive work on language and gender. Through the study of texts with more than one writer, especially when they are by writers of different genders and ages, students can develop their understanding of the relationship between female and male voices. This activity also introduces students to the idea of writing commentaries, a skill demanded in the coursework component of the course.

Read the following problem and response from *Sugar* magazine's website. There are of course many other problem pages that can be found to use as additional resources for these lessons. Discuss the nature of the problem; the language that Kelly uses to describe herself, her relationship and her partner; the relationship between the two voices in the text; the way that Kelly's problem is answered by a male writer; the relationship of authority between this example and the notion of people offering readers advice in general.

He's taking advantage

Q:
I recently moved in with my boyfriend. We were both planning to get jobs and split the bills, but now I'm doing two jobs and he's unemployed and spends all day playing computer games. I love him, but I don't like him treating me like this. Help!
Kelly, 18, Hull

A:
One of the biggest problems with being in love is that the strength of your emotions makes it harder for you to be completely rational about what's going on with you and your boyfriend. You need to take a step back. Would you let this lad treat you like this if you weren't in love with him? Or would you ever treat someone you loved like this? I think your boyfriend is living the easy life at your expense. Talk to him. If he refuses to change then the harsh truth is that you're better off without him.

Figure 8: Boyfriend trouble

Source: www.sugarmagazine.co.uk

This can easily fill a lesson and whilst there is enough material here for the students to write an essay, responding to this text with their own creative writing is potentially a far more rewarding learning experience.

TASK

1　Ask students to write their own letter to a problem page. This should be done in a way that emulates the tone of these types of letters, and not for comedic effect.
2　Take in the letters and redistribute around the group so that each letter can be given a response from another student.
3　Take time to share letters and responses, this can be most entertaining, but the discussion should be refocused so that the students are analysing the texts and responses for their authenticity. In their commentaries the students will not need to comment on the responses, but it is still a worthwhile exercise.

4   Using your knowledge of the coursework mark scheme, teach students how to write a short commentary that explains the decisions that they made when writing the letter.

5   Get the students to reproduce this work neatly, and use as display work that will become a resource when writing the real coursework pieces.

Defining gender

Much work has been done by dictionary editors and academics alike to attempt to define gendered lexical items and gendered concepts. By continuing to consider theoretical notions of gender alongside close textual analysis of texts that are interesting in this area of the course your students' understanding will flourish.

Here are seven definitions of gendered terms. The list is easy to adapt and we would encourage you to take this approach.

1   Man: i.   an adult human male

ii.   a human being of either sex; a person.

2   Woman: an adult human female

3   Male: of or denoting the sex which produces gametes, especially spermatozoa, with which a female may be fertilised or inseminated to produce offspring.

4   Female: of or denoting the sex that can bear offspring that can bear offspring or produce eggs, distinguished biologically by the production of gametes (ova) which can be fertilised by male gametes.

All definitions from the OED

5   'One is not born a woman – but rather becomes one', *The Second Sex* by Simone de Beauvoir.

6   'In 'woman' I see something that cannot be represented, something that is not said, something above and beyond nomenclatures and ideologies', Julia Kristeva.

7   'One is one's gender to the extent that one is not the other gender', *Gender Trouble* by Judith Butler.

What to do with these quotations.

1.   Read them together and share what you understand by them.

2.   Do you agree that it is possible to define these terms?

3.   Re-read your piece of homework, and others', that I have just returned and reconsider some of the views presented.

4.   Write your own definitions of the terms:

Gender

Woman

Man

Again, because this material is so simple to develop and adapt this can easily be extended to at least two hours of lessons. The fourth task (writing the definitions) is particularly difficult and it is worthwhile spending time developing the writing skills required to complete it.

Musical representations of gender

George Jones and Tammy Wynette are two of Country Music's greatest artists. They married in 1969 and after some dangerously good times they divorced in 1975. Both are recognised as fine solo artists and they also recorded many songs together. These lessons use the lyrics of two of their songs, both clearly from the perspective of the gender group to which they belong.

Tammy Wynette grew up on the farm where she was born in Mississippi in 1933. She was raised by her mother and grandparents after her father died when she was only eight months old. George Jones was born in Saratoga, Texas on 12 September 1931. At age 12 he was already earning money playing music. By the time he was 21, he had served in the Marines; when he left the Marines in 1952. He painted houses for a living. In his spare time Jones sang and played music.

The songs are deliberately taken from a field of music that your students probably don't listen to. Aside from opening their ears to something that they have never heard this decision allows you to transcend musical preferences and to study texts objectively. It is, of course, preferable that you download the songs in order for phonological aspects of the songs to be felt and explained alongside the linguistic analysis that will be conducted on the written texts.

Look at the texts in terms of:

Language choices to describe the other sex
The emotions that each song reveals
Attitudes to relationships
Use of imagery and what that says about gender.

This can be used as a starting point of research in to attitudes to gender in music. It can be developed by setting your students independent research projects to discover how genders are represented in different genres of music. For example, they could research how attitudes to women are shown in hip hop, whether there are differences between attitudes in music from 40 years ago to now, whether it is possible to discover if a song is written by a woman or a man. The possibilities are endless and these research projects will allow your students to look at familiar areas of contemporary life through the eyes of a linguist.

Here is one final text for analysis. Sex and relationships are always a crowd-pleaser in A level lessons. Use this not only to gain attention but also to demonstrate that the keenest linguists will be using their skills of analysis throughout their days and when looking at everyday texts. Linguistic analysis isn't just for lessons. The source is www.menshealth.co.uk/sex/please-woman/get-your-own-way-9433.

Texts directed at a specific gender of reader are always rich ground for analysis. A word of caution before we start. Examination boards do not always choose such explicitly gendered texts for analysis in exams. You also need to source less obvious texts and the best starting point for this is past papers from your exam board. To attract teenagers' eyes, however, the *Men's Health* example is excellent.

This is a text designed to inform, entertain and persuade a male reader. The audience is probably aged between 18 and 45; there is a high probability that they are predominantly heterosexual too. Like any gender-specific magazine, there is a likelihood that it would be read by members of the other sex too.

Get your own way

Four fool-proof ways to make sure you get what you want

Listen

"Listening is the very first thing", says Dr Elizabeth Mapstone, chartered psychologist and author of *War of Words* (Vintage, £6.99). "You must find out where the other person is coming from so you know how to couch your argument." If you listen carefully, you may discover that she doesn't object to you going to the darts match in itself, just not on your anniversary ... that you forgot about.

Find common ground

And go and stand on it together. "You don't have to lie. There will always be something you can genuinely agree on", says Mapstone. Like: Yes, in an ideal world everybody probably would clear up after themselves. No, we don't live in an ideal world. Look, you're on common ground already.

Negotiate a win/win

"Don't beat people into a corner", says Ben Williams, Edinburgh-placed chartered psychologist. "If you completely flatten someone, whatever you win from them will come grudgingly, or late, or more expensively. The best negotiations make both parties happy, so you both look out for each other's interests willingly."

Don't gloat

Pointing a finger and saying, "Nerny nerny ner ner" makes it more difficult for them to concede gracefully next time. "Congratulate your negotiating partner on what a hard bargain you drove instead", says Williams.

There are many assumptions made in this text. It attempts to take a light-hearted approach to the subject. Whether you and your students agree with this is up for debate, but it seems arguable that this is not an article that takes itself too seriously. That is not to say that the article doesn't represent serious issues that need to be discussed. The title, 'Get Your Own Way' is immediately interesting in its depiction of gender relations. There is a hint of antagonism here, and power struggle. This embedded assertion that relationships are about gaining the upper hand on your loved one creates a slightly uncomfortable (or ironic/comedic) tone. There is vagueness in the grammatical construction which creates this uncertainty. Either a declarative statement in itself or an abbreviated form of '(How to) Get Your Own Way', the sentence implies that what follows are instructions that will enable you to gain superior status in your relationship. Further analysis of grammatical constructions throughout the piece will allow you and your students to explore this detail further.

Graphologically, the piece barely conceals the underlying benefits of following the advice being offered. The image is very powerful. It suggests to men in a relationship that there will most definitely be physical reward for being in the ascendency. The layout of the four short, sub-titled paragraphs develops this. The titles are immediately recognisable and offer the reader a simply structured text. The ultimate effect of these graphological choices is to state that harmony and physical pleasures are only four simple steps away.

In the written text, the editorial voice is barely present at all; it is the voices of experts that we hear. Two chartered psychologists provide simple and direct advice. Within these guidelines for success are hidden assumptions about both genders. These assumptions, or dare I say stereotypes are as follows, divided into sections as the article is.

Listen
- Men don't listen
- Women complain about men going out.

Find common ground
- Men lie and are untidy
- Women complain about men lying and being untidy.

Negotiate a win/win
- Men are aggressive
- Women are passive.

Don't Gloat
- Men gloat.

This list is subjective, but it does offer a way in to the exploration of how gender relations can be explored by pulling up the corner of the rug and seeing what lies beneath.

When studying language and gender stress caution at all times. It becomes very tempting for us as teachers and our students to let our subjectivities guide our readings. This is fine, as long as we continue to be explicitly aware of it.

Language and power

Language and power is a topic that gets your students' analytical skills targeted towards some of the most significant questions they will engage with on the course. Power is a rich and fascinating area for study and it can be found throughout the course as an embedded feature of many texts. There are three questions that will provide a consistent analytical approach when exploring this area of English.

- Where does power reside?
- How is power encoded linguistically?
- How can we respond to the power exerted through language?

Advertisers attempt to exert power in their attempts to get us to spend our money on their clients' products. Journalists can be seen as playing a role that empowers their readers – we become more confident, more knowledgeable and more socially aware. Charities often try to make the reader feel empowered by stating that we can change lives and environments by donating. Power is also demonstrated more explicitly in legal documents such as court summons or parliamentary Acts. In notices about parking restrictions, demands for payment from service providers, rule books published by sporting bodies, instructions how to assemble new furniture, power is exerted for different reasons and in different ways.

Collecting texts is an easy thing to do when teaching this section of the course. They are everywhere. You can take photographs of signs, collect adverts, articles and comment pages from magazines and newspapers. Reviews of products, services, books, theatre productions, games and television shows all reveal a writer's power. Legal documentation, transcribed conversations and scripted talk are further sources of rich text for analysis.

Four examples of different types of discourse with accompanying analysis are given below. They demonstrate power in different ways and act as demonstrations of how you and your students can collect texts that can be used for discussion in your classroom.

Explicit power: secondary school prospectus

BEHAVIOUR

Discipline is central to the whole learning process and without it nothing worthwhile socially or educationally can be achieved, and we expect the support of all parents. We each have a responsibility to share in creating an environment at Woodlands where people matter. Above all SELF DISCIPLINE is that achievement to which we should all aspire.

We expect behaviour of the highest standard in and out of the classroom; to and from school. Everyone at Woodlands is required to behave in a civilised manner and not prevent, by their behaviour, other members of our community from functioning properly.

We will not tolerate bullying, racism, vandalism, hooliganism, illegal items, illegal substances, illegal practices or bad language.

A guide for parents and students explaining our behaviour expectations and our response to unacceptable behaviour is included in the student planner.

Source: www.woodlands.derby.sch.uk/documents/Prospectus2010.pdf

A school prospectus has to tread a very fine line in the ways that it exerts and concedes power. The interactional context between school and parent means that the school needs to demonstrate some of its power over its students and parents whilst acknowledging the parents' rights to choose any one of a number of schools for their child. The school must set out its rules and expectations whilst offering a welcoming and purposeful environment; it must demonstrate control over children's behaviour whilst offering an open environment in which learners can flourish. These tensions are not always counter to one another – as we see in this extract.

Lexical choices have been made to suggest a balance between control and expectations. 'Discipline', 'behaviour', 'highest standard', 'tolerate' and 'unacceptable' all contribute to the semantic field of authority that a school has. These lexical choices clearly state that the senior leadership team, in partnership with the school's governing body, has the power to decide where the boundaries of appropriate and inappropriate behaviour lie. They imply that the school has the power to make judgements of what is 'unacceptable' and that those judgements should be respected by students and parents. In paragraph three the list of prohibited acts secures the school's authority by juxtaposing their own decisions with those that are backed by external powers: the phrases 'Illegal items', 'illegal substances' and 'illegal practices' could be supported by government legislation; listing 'illegal' things alongside the school's own non-accepted behaviours raising the status of the latter, as they appear to coexist with the law.

Grammatical decisions are made to reinforce the semantic field of discipline. 'We' is used five times. This choice of first-person plural pronoun creates a sense of inclusion whilst also creating an impersonal voice. In most instances 'we' is the school's authority, the individuals who will make significant decisions on misconduct. Where it is used in the phrase 'We each have a responsibility' the text exerts power by including the reader in the 'we', ensuring that parental responsibility is encoded in the school's beliefs.

Further ways of exerting power are exercised, at times reaching beyond the institution's limits and beyond those prescribed by law. The phrase 'civilised manner' reaches out to a discourse of culture. The definition of 'civilised behaviour' is culturally encoded, it reaches past semantics and pragmatics. Ideology is at work here; the school prospectus needs ideological power to state its ultimate message.

Encourage your students to write what this means – it is an incredibly difficult thing to do, especially in our multi-ethnic, multi-faith and multi-cultural society. Does it mean anything at all?

Transferred power – Sustrans

About Sustrans

Sustrans is the UK's leading sustainable transport charity. Our vision is a world in which people choose to travel in ways that benefit their health and the environment. Every day we are working on practical, innovative ways of dealing with the transport challenges that affect us all. Sustrans aims to:

- reduce the environmental and resource impacts of transport
- enable people to choose active travel more often
- provide car-free access to essential local services
- turn streets and public spaces into places for people to enjoy.

We work in three ways to achieve these aims:

- we create public space focussed on access not mobility
- we provide information and work directly with people to bring about behaviour change
- we influence government policy by demonstrating that it is possible to change people's behaviour and by measuring the benefit of our work in terms of health, environment, quality of life and value for money.

Source: www.sustrans.org.uk/about-sustrans [accessed 27 June 2010].

Charities are organisations that have to encourage people to support their cause. This can be done either by persuading people to be financial donors to support their work or to act in ways that complements the work that the charity undertakes. Either way, their literature needs to do two things. First, charities must convince people that the work they do changes governmental policies and people's actions or belief systems. Second, they need to convince people that by supporting them, individuals can become agents of change.

Sustrans is a charity whose aims are to change attitudes and behaviour towards travel. One of their most significant projects is the creation of cycle routes, allowing us the freedom to travel safely by bike. Their literature, exemplified by the above extract from their website, attempts to empower their readers and contributors by offering aims and arguments that direct their attempts to exert influence on the world.

The sense of empowerment is central to the successful communications of the organisation's aims here. Throughout the extract an impression is created that Sustrans is an agent of change and its supporters are also making significant contributions to changing the world. Here the semantic field creates a sense of a clean environment and freedom. 'Sustainable', 'health', 'environment' and 'transport' all contribute to the field of healthy travel and 'active', 'enjoy', 'public space' and 'quality of life' create a sense of the envisaged freedom that will benefit us all if their aims are achieved.

The idea of transferred power is an important one here. Sustrans is the organisation trying to augment change. They do this practically by making cycle routes and politically by lobbying government to change policy. They transfer power by creating opportunities for everyone in the country to participate in cycling and by raising awareness of its health and environmental benefits. They also do this linguistically.

The semantic field has already been identified and it can be argued that this is, in itself, an act of transferring power to the reader. By participating in a lifestyle which provides senses of freedom and change the reader is given this power by Sustrans. Let us examine some grammatical constructions to see if a full linguistic analysis bears this initial finding out.

In its aims the charity states that it will try to 'enable people to choose active travel more often'. The verb choice, in its infinitive form 'to choose' places the power to make decisions in the mind of the reader. Transference of power involves an organisation's agency being handed over to individuals and groups; this is very clearly happening here and it is coded in the grammar of the aim. Coupled with the noun phrase 'active travel' the choice seems ever more powerful. The reader's thoughts are now in the sphere of activity or passivity, and it can be argued that the effects of the grammar are potentially life-changing. This push for society to become more active – which is clearly a more desirable state in the view of the charity – is embedded further in the aim to 'turn streets and public spaces into places for people to enjoy.' Enjoyment now, as well as all the previously-mentioned benefits is once again offered as a verb in its infinitive form. This bold statement suggests that Sustrans is an organisation whose power is best exerted when it is transferred to individual participants and the wider community.

The power of expertise

The power relationships in your own classrooms are intriguing sources for contemplation and discussion. As teachers we notice interplay of power and lack of it in the relationships between the students we teach. This is sensitive ground for discussion, and maybe one to avoid confronting directly, but it is there and your students will be all too aware of the flux and flow of power in their worlds. The power that teachers have is a subject to take on in lessons and it can be considered under the heading of the power of expertise.

Expertise manifests itself in many ways in our world. Tradespeople and professionals are experts in fields such as plumbing or investment banking. Scholars in higher education establishments often take expertise to its limits, becoming massively knowledgeable about, and devoting life's work to sometimes very precise areas of study. Equally, your students will be expert about subjects from their worlds. Dubstep, mountaineering, caring for family members, dance, kick-boxing, *The OC*; all of these and countless more are areas of expertise that some of my students have acquired at levels way above my knowledge of them. What teachers definitely have are two areas of expertise beyond that of their students, for now, at least. They are education itself and the specific subject taught. So, you are the expert in the room about linguistics and how to teach it. You have the power. Let us explore an extract of an art teacher speaking to his students, first to the whole class then the dialogue shifts to being more closely intended for one student. What is said is audible to all students throughout. We are in a KS3 classroom in an inner city, comprehensive secondary school. The teacher is also a School Director.

> T: Still a little bit too noisy if I'm honest. Right I'm going to let you into a secret – tricks of the trade – if you're drawing something that's very complicated, okay I've just told Courtney this, have a go at looking at the biggest or the most simple shape you can and in a lot of these shells' cases, okay, it might be that I'm gonna draw over these, it might be a spiral like that, okay not exactly like that you don't have to get it exactly like that. Some of them have got little shapes coming off of them, yeah and they get bigger, don't they? Right so have a look and try and break it down. Hannah you've got a spiral but yours is slightly different yours goes yours goes big, really quickly like that, but it's still a spiral. Yeah? And then you can get, after you've done that you can get all of those patterns going like that on it, have a go. Yeah? Can't fault yourself.
>
> *Recorded during January 2009*

Let's start from the top down on this one. What we have is an extract of a longer piece of discourse, edited down to be a similar length to an extract your students may be offered in their examination at the end of the year. There are many ways in which power is demonstrated and exerted. The declaration that it is 'a little bit noisy in here' is a familiar phrase to teachers and students; power over young people's behaviour is shown. Letting the students in to 'a secret' demonstrates expertise over subject-matter; power over young people's acquisition of skills is exerted. In the direct and public address to Hannah knowledge of an individual's work is displayed; power related to student progress is exerted and the power to motivate is shown in the closing phrases 'have a go' and '(c)an't fault yourself.' In one short extract the power that resides in expertise is demonstrated in a variety of different ways. The art teacher is in control of the classroom and this is shown in ways other than the explicit control of volume. He appears relaxed, as shown in the informality of his tone. He knows students' names and their work and uses this knowledge to explore ways of becoming successful in producing art. He is also in possession of knowledge that he is keen to share. All of these features of the discourse guide a linguist's eye towards a reading that power in this text clearly resides with the teacher and the ways in which that power is demonstrated leads to successful interaction with his students.

With those views about discourse shared, you can now set your students to work on further linguistic frameworks to add depth and vigour to the initial reading. Rather than go through a sequence of readings here, let us take some time, in a moment, to consider the writing skills needed to succeed in the examination. Before that there is the final model of power to look at.

Institutional power

An institution is best thought of as an organisation or body with an important position in society. The word carries other connotations too and that semantic play is relevant here. Governments and Assemblies are the institutions in our society that carry the most power and we can look to the example from the Welsh Assembly to explore how this power is encoded in the language it uses to communicate with the Welsh people. The text below is BBC Cymru and explains, in English and Welsh, some basic details about the institutions.

Representing Wales and its people

The Assembly is made up of 60 elected *Assembly Members*, who represent a specific area of Wales as a member of a *political party* (Conservative, Labour, Liberal Democrat, Plaid Cymru) or as an independent member (not a member of the four main political parties).
The *Welsh government* is formed following an *Assembly election*, and is composed of up to 14 *Assembly Members*.

Cynrychioli Cymru a'i phobl
Mae'r *Cynulliad* yn cynnwys 60 o *Aelodau Cynulliad* etholedig, sy'n cynrychioli arda-loedd penodol yng Nghymru, a hynny fel aelod o *bleidiau gwleidyddol* (Y Ceidwadwyr Cymreig, Llafur, y Democratiaid Rhyddfrydol a Phlaid Cymru) neu fel aelodau annib-ynnol (heb fod yn aelod o un o'r pedair prif blaid wleidyddol).
Caiff *Llywodraeth Cymru* ei ffurfio ar ôl cynnal *etholiad Cynulliad*, ac mae'n cynnwys hyd at 14 o *Aelodau Cynulliad*.

Using the top–down approach again, let's look at where power resides in the discourse and then explore how to write about these features, along with semantics and grammar, as we get to the end of this section.

The piece is declarative and formal in tone; throughout the article the writers have taken the choice to make the information seem as impersonal and institutional as they can. The effect is an authoritative piece of writing which successfully manages to leave the reader more fully informed about the nature and purpose of the Welsh Assembly. The text appears twice within a single piece of discourse – in English then in Welsh. There are power implications here. The history of power struggle between the two nations is too lengthy to discuss here, and wouldn't be directly relevant to our linguistic exploration; it is perhaps enough to say that the political equilibrium demonstrated by Wales being a genuinely dual language nation shows how a fight to regain power lost/taken over the centuries is something that is possible. As a feature of the discourse, it is directly relevant, as it shows readers, students and politicians in England that cultural dominance is not a permanent obstruction, but one that can be removed following years of struggle. Capitalisation of key terms throughout adds to the effect and hyperlinks are suggestive that many of the terms are important enough to require further detailing in a glossary.

To add to the explanations offered here and to explore how to write about language and power the final part of this section deals with writing. Rather than a complete essay, it is a model of how to enable your students to build up small analytical points so that they become a substantial reading.

I will return to the teacher discourse first. Below is a copy of the extract which has been highlighted for semantic field, in a way similar to your students' work in the classroom.

> T: Still a little bit too <u>noisy</u> if I'm honest. Right I'm going to let you into a secret – tricks of the trade – if you're <u>drawing</u> something that's very complicated, okay I've just told Courtney this, have a go at looking at the biggest or the most <u>simple shape</u> you can and in a lot of these shells' cases, okay, it might be that I'm gonna <u>draw</u> over these, it might be <u>a spiral</u> like that, okay not exactly like that you don't have to get it exactly like that. Some of them have got <u>little shapes</u> coming off of them, yeah and <u>they get bigger</u>, don't they? Right so have a look and try and <u>break it down</u>. Hannah you've got <u>a spiral</u> but yours is slightly different yours goes <u>yours goes big</u>, really quickly like that, but it's still <u>a spiral</u>. Yeah? And then you can get, after you've done that you can get all of <u>those patterns</u> going like that on it, have a go. Yeah? Can't fault yourself.
>
> *Recording made during January 2009*

The highlighted words act as notes for a section of writing about semantic field. First, we need a sentence to capture the observation.

1   When talking to his class the teacher uses the semantic field of drawing to enable his students to understand the process that he is teaching them.

This sentence indicates to an examiner how a linguistic framework has been analysed and related to the overall purpose of the text. It is concise and accurate and serves as a foundation on which to build precise details.

2   The repetition of the lexical item 'spiral' serves to closely focus the students' attention on the key feature of the objects being studied. The teacher does this in order to attract their attention to this feature, as doing so will allow them to see what is most important. By doing this he can also demonstrate his skill as a teacher and artist.

This development takes a quotation from the text and uses it to add some detail to the claim made in the first sentence. Linguistic awareness is shown by doing this as the point is starting to relate semantic field to power.

3   By subtly reassuring his students of his artistic skill the teacher exerts power by enabling his students to achieve an illustration better than one undertaken without instruction. Other terms from this semantic field complement this move; 'little shapes', 'break it down' and 'those patterns' create an air of sophistication. The activity they are being instructed in has its own language; the teacher uses this language whilst also communicating in a way that is comprehensible to KS3 students.

Now there is the beginning of a coherent analysis. By building up from small observations to bigger claims your students will see how their skills as readers can be transformed into skills as writers.

In the text about the Welsh Assembly, grammatical choices are made that relate closely to the overall purpose of the text. This in turn is closely linked to the ways that power is exerted and described.

> 1   The declarative grammatical construction used in all of the sentences is a significant factor in the way this informative text is composed.

This opener is a precise reading of the sentences in the piece. It demonstrates understanding of grammar and how to link observations to purpose. It needs to be built upon.

> 2   Paragraphs one and two, which begin, 'The Assembly is made up of' and 'The Welsh Government is formed' are examples of the declarative structure. These are definitive statements, they are factual and their tone leaves the reader feeling informed. The use of the definite article at the beginning of each sentence is important here – it establishes the sole focus of the writing. It also elevates the status of the Assembly by making it the singular subject of the sentences.

It doesn't take much to build up small insights into detailed sentences. Your students may not create polished items in the early stages of the course. They need to acquire this skill through practice and your teaching and this will happen. Starting early in the course with short and undaunting tasks will ensure that they are well-developed writers by the time the exams arrive.

Language and technology

Pre-teaching thinking

I think that there are two overriding considerations relevant to this section.

First, the technology that you will be discussing changes so fast that it is very difficult to transfer your resources and materials from one year to the next. Much of the writing and thinking that has gone on in this area is already out-of-date. As new technologies evolve and then make their way into common usage, the impact that they create on the language changes too. The range of possibilities for language transaction broadens. This means a growth in the potential for those transactions, limited only by the capabilities of the particular device. Therefore, this subject is always fresh. It really does suit the investigative approach. Collection of raw data is valuable here. There is also a great deal of debate in the media about the ways in which technology is affecting our society and in particular young people. Clearly, your students are well placed to join this debate.

Secondly, technology is an area that students are very interested in. Young people today have a great expectation of what technology can do for them. Most are highly skilled in the different forms of communication available to them. The language of technology is not fixed in the way that Standard English has become. This allows a great deal of freedom to create forms and conventions. People are inventing words, phrases, keyboard conventions and voices that did not previously exist.

The new modes of communicating are really accelerating the rate of change in the English language. A few years ago, a whole new opening to conversational discourse came about because of the advent of the mobile phone. It became necessary to ask where the person that you had called was. Perhaps alongside this we had a shift in the level of trust that people could invest in telephone usage. The person at the other end could tell you they were anywhere! That is not the fault of the telephone but you take my point about the ways in which options are opening up.

More recently, social networking has become a topical issue. Taking facebook as an example, it has become possible to maintain 'contact' with people you know, in my case my aunt and uncle in Canada, without seeing or hearing them. I can have access to their photos and they can have access to mine. I can 'talk' to them, typing in messages and receiving almost instantaneous responses. This is all very useful but the immediacy and accessibility of internet communication has created a very real fear of misuse. Young people are vulnerable in their desire to have as many 'Friends' as possible on their profile page. They often feel the need to appear popular. This can lead to them allowing free access to their details and to their acceptance of people that they do not know. Again, the trustworthiness of the medium is called into question.

Idea one: A project to get started

How about starting with an investigation! Here are four possible titles for your students to consider.

1   Is it true that people of different ages have different ways of using language when text messaging?
2   Having collected all my incoming and outgoing text messages for a week, what conclusions can I come to about the role text messaging plays in my life?
3   Has my use of facebook (etc. ...) expanded or contracted my social life?
4   What, if any, are the differences in the ways that I employ written language at school and in my personal life?

Often, teachers can be a little wary of the internet for research. However, with these sorts of enquiry it is clearly essential; not only for collecting data but also for reading the debate about text, bebo, msn, facebook etc. It is a debate that is largely being carried out on the internet, and in the pages of newspapers and their websites and blogs.

You could make use of this project as practice towards the investigative coursework at A2. If you were to follow the structure noted below for the written feedback, it would be a rehearsal for the structure of the longer piece in Year 13.

1   *Introduction* – discusses the area of linguistics to be investigated.
2   *Aims* – a discussion of the task set and perhaps a hypothesis.
3   *Methodology* – step-by-step guide to the collection of data including ways in which the student has tried to make the testing fair.
4   *Findings and analysis* – individual points that have been discovered.
5   *Conclusions* – a direct answer to the question that students posed themselves.
6   *Evaluation* – a consideration of the value of the project given size of sample and the data collected.

It is important that students value what they do here as it can be mentioned in examination answers. Their collection of data is real and, obviously, up-to-date. They must be clear that they are research linguists and that what they have found out will be treated as valuable, just as valuable as published findings. Remember, this is an area in constant change. The research out there is probably becoming dated anyway. It is not always easy for students to accept that their work has authority. In this case, as long as the testing is reasonable, the research is definitely valid and worth a mention in exam answers. It demonstrates an active linguist with an enquiring mind.

Idea two: Technical ways in which language changes because of technology

Another way of approaching this subject is to return to your basic frameworks and see how texts produced with new technology are throwing up new and interesting features.

Here are some examples.

GRAMMAR

Here is a text message in which the writer is organising a game of football.

> 8.30 start 2nite. Game
> Is def ON, jjb rang to
> confirm. C u there

In terms of grammar, this text works in a number of ways outside Standard grammatical forms. Each 'sentence' makes use of contractions. The number 2 is used as part of a word and the letters c and u represent words through the sound that they make. The capitalisation of the word ON increases the sense of definiteness. There is no final full stop to indicate an ending and there is no use of a sender name or salutation to the receiver.

Technology has played a large part in the formation of this communication. The writer is actively crafting his text to suit the form/mode of communication. Texts cost money, long texts normally cost more than short texts. This financial consideration has meant the advent of various ways of communicating in a shorthand version of the language. The number of the writer is communicated to the receiver on their device and the name is probably pre-saved so name and number no longer seem like requirements of a communication. The final full stop would add nothing in terms of the message and is therefore missed out. The only reason that capitals have been used at the start of the sentences is because the phone automatically puts the capital in. The sports company JJB would in Standard English require capitalisation but here the writer chooses not to bother.

You can open the debate about the merits of writing in this way. Is this type of writing lazy and inarticulate? Or, maybe it demonstrates a playful inventiveness with language?

A further activity that you could do with this text is to give a long-hand version to your students and ask them individually to 'convert' it into text speak. The long-hand version might read something like this.

Dear Ben,
The game tonight kicks off at 8.30. JJB rang me earlier to confirm that the game will definitely be on. I will see you there.
Martin

Hopefully, your students will be able to make adaptations that will support the idea that texts are shortened as a general rule. It might also turn out that there are various different ways of doing this activity. This can lead into a discussion about the fact that everyone is making up their own rules about how to text. Sometimes, we individually use different conventions to write to different people. This opens up the idea of the lack of rules in this form of communication. Is this liberating or confusing for the writers and receivers? Another good discussion topic.

LEXICAL CHOICES/SEMANTICS

A whole new vocabulary is growing, and will continue to grow, around the new technologies. New modes of communication require neologisms to help to identify and name the new ways of communicating. There are a number of ways that we can classify the types of new words that have entered the language. This is applicable to all areas of new language generation.

- *Loan words* – have generally been 'borrowed' from other languages. I always find this definition somewhat misleading as we are certainly not going to give the word back!
- *Creations (or Neologisms) – brand new words.* These are rare but they do sometimes appear. It is often very hard to identify when and where these words first appeared.
- *Meaning shifts.* When words shift in meaning to encompass a new meaning. Sometimes the original meaning might disappear but more often an extra nuance is added to the word.
- *Blending.* This is where two already existent words join together, using a portion of both. An example would be *motel* being part *hotel* and part *motor*.
- *Compounds.* This is where two existing words join to create a new concept. An example would be the use of *lap* and *top* to form *laptop*.
- *Shortenings (acronyms)* Here words are formed from initial letters, sometimes pronounced/readable as a single word, as in radar or fifa, and sometimes the letters are sounded out individually, as in RSPCA or DNA.

virus
disk
netiquette
megadrive
SGML
user-friendly
cyberspace
desktop
mouse
e-commerce

It can be helpful to your students to try to identify the ways that our language adapts to characterise the new inventions that are being developed.

Here is a handy list that you might use in class to see if your students can sift and sort the new vocabulary of technology.

You could make use of the types of language change as headings and ask your students to put these words in the right columns. A development of this activity is obviously to get your students to collect their own examples of the ways in which vocabulary is developing to fill this need.

There are scores of fascinating words that can be tracked in terms of their recent etymology. Take, for example, the word 'reboot'. What does it mean and how does it make use of its two constituent parts *re-* and *boot*? There are loads of examples that your students will be able to track down and investigate. What is meant by *virtual reality* and, again, how has this new expression made use of the original denotative and connotative values of each of the words? Whilst something like *laptop* is really straightforward, *online* will open up a rich vein of investigation.

Here are some more words you could investigate, either collectively or individually: radar, scuba, NATO, HTML, JPEG, URL, palmtop, floppy, PC, RAM, debugging, defragging, resetting, internaut and snail mail.

In a funny way, in looking at the newness of the language you can trace the links that we make with the language that we already have. Your students will gain a good appreciation of the incremental nature of our language.

Idea three: How has the advent of New Media changed the producer–receiver relationship?

When listening to Talksport Radio, as I am wont to do when cooking, I can often feel the need to join in with the various debates that are taking place. Something that has been said may have made me angry or I may feel moved to add to the sentiment of the speaker. The advent of the mobile phone means that I can instantaneously communicate with the broadcasters and often my communication will be read out and some kind of feedback will be given. This is a serious change in the way that the traditional media forms of radio and television operate. No longer do they benefit from a sense of authority and power and distance that requires that I sit at home and fume or smile at what has been said. The programmer can still choose to edit the thoughts of the audience but they are certainly going to be aware of how their audience feels about the output that they have produced. I often feel the need to give my editorial comments to what is going on. I regularly note the inflammatory tone of the phone-in programmes that invite people to be racist or sexist. I feel empowered, in a way that I would not have been ten years ago, to text in and express my displeasure and let the producer know that I know what they are up to. The impact that my comment has is probably minimal but what has changed is the ease of access that makes me feel that I can contribute. I would never phone a radio station (too shy!), I would not send them a letter (too much like hard work) and I would not send them an email (disproportionate effort to value of the time spent writing it) but the sheer ease and immediacy of a text encourages me to join in. It is the mode of communication that has empowered me to take part. If it were not for the ease of the communication and the anticipation of instant feedback of being named on the radio, then I would not bother. What is particularly noteworthy here is the way in which I have become part of the broadcast, whether I contribute or not. The potential for my joining in is there and this changes the way that I view the communication of a radio programme. This idea of interactivity is one that you could open up to your students. They may well take this option for granted. If you are able to indicate the one-way transaction of language that television and radio used to be, students might well be able to trace the developments in the media and consider in what ways the audience's role has changed.

Idea four: Social networking

This is the current area of interest. Here the line between producer and receiver becomes somewhat blurred. Everyone can have a site and become a publisher. Musicians can advertise their music on myspace. On facebook, any and everyone can become a writer. You can organise the content of your profile and you can write on the wall of other people's areas. You can become the creator of interest groups that garner interest from all over the world. People that you never knew existed can join your site and begin to communicate with you. You are able to decide the levels of access that people can have to your information and you can regulate the material that you publish. Suddenly, everyone is a writer! Do you think that your students take this for granted? Maybe so. They need to know that this represents an explosion in the area of life known as publishing.

Perhaps you could gather together the groups that your students have initiated on facebook and the like to see how they are making use of such sites to express their own interests. Could you lead a discussion about the perceived values of such sites?

Idea five: Fun with emoticons!

Making use of the computer keyboard, invite your students to design their own new emoticons.

Here is mine   ; > (winking devilish grin)

I know that it is a bit rubbish but that fact in itself might encourage your students to come up with something better. Whilst doing this activity your students will learn for themselves the ways in which the communications that we wish to make are limited by the mode itself. This could lead to a wider discussion of the ways other media limit what is possible.

An article from the BBC website:

Online networking 'harms health'

People's health could be harmed by social networking sites because they reduce levels of face-to-face contact, an expert claims. Dr Aric Sigman says websites such as Facebook set out to enrich social lives, but end up keeping people apart. A lack of 'real' social networking, involving personal interaction, may have biological effects, he suggests. He also says that evidence suggests that a lack of face-to-face networking could alter the way genes work, upset immune responses, hormone levels, the function of arteries, and influence mental performance. This, he claims, could increase the risk of health problems as serious as cancer, strokes, heart disease, and dementia.

'Evolutionary mechanism'

Dr Sigman maintains that social networking sites have played a significant role in making people become more isolated. 'Social networking sites should allow us to embellish our social lives, but what we find is very different'. Dr Sigman says that there is research that suggests the number of hours people spend interacting face-to-face has fallen dramatically since 1987, as the use of electronic media has increased. He claims that interacting 'in person' has an effect on the body that is not seen when e-mails are written. 'When we are "really" with people different things happen', he said. 'It's probably an evolutionary mechanism that recognises the benefits of us being together geographically. Much of it isn't understood, but there does seem to be a difference between "real presence" and the virtual variety.' Dr Sigman also argues using electronic media undermines people's social skills and their ability to read body language. 'One of the most pronounced changes in the daily habits of British citizens is a reduction in the number of minutes per day that they interact with another human being', he said. 'In less than two decades, the number of people saying there is no-one with whom they discuss important matters nearly tripled.'

Dr Sigman says he is 'worried about where this is all leading'.

A SELECTION OF THE COMMENTS TO THE BBC WEBSITE:

I agree that I would prefer face-to-face contact with my friends and family, but as an immigrant to the UK who is separated from so many friends and family far away in another country and as a disabled person with a variable health condition that means that some days I am unable to get out of bed, the internet and social networking is a real lifeline for me. Losing track of old friends can happen so easily. I've re-established many friendships this way.

Just a week ago I switched off my facebook account for just this reason. These sites claim greater social networking, but all it really creates are more distractions for people, more isolation in front of their computers, more escapism, and a false sense of relationships with other people. People do not interact with each other properly, becoming more isolated and so more depressed.

I live in a very rural community that unfortunately is seriously lacking in community spirit. There is very, very little to do and very little social interaction. I do not drive and I am home with small children. If it weren't for facebook I would feel even more isolated from society than I already am. Facebook reminds me that there are people out there who care about me, even though they may be people I grew up with that live thousands of miles away.

I use most of the social networking sites that there are. I live in a small village where nobody talks to each other in person. I've tried everything to create human interaction and even done a School for Social Entrepreneurs Course to assist me in that but to no avail. I know that online friends are not the same but I am a single parent and not working. It is the only social interaction I can get to drive away the loneliness. When people are not online I miss them.

I couldn't agree more. I witness my four year-old-son and his eight year-old sister interact wonderfully when playing together, yet they become 'withdrawn' and subdued when playing solitary electronic games. Technology should enhance the human experience, but often fails to live up to its brief and actually causes more harm compared to when we did without.

Idea six: online articles

So we have seen from the BBC article, that we have edited somewhat, the possible effects of social networking websites, first looking at the article itself and next at a number of responses left by those who read the article. As a resource this can be very useful for investigating the current worry about the impact of new modes of communication. Many such articles on the subject can be found on the internet.

You could give students the article first and ask them to consider the two main areas of concern that are proposed: namely damage to physical health and the isolating effect. I am sure that your group might well feel that they are able to keep in touch with more people through the medium of social networking sites. The second part, the responses, might increase awareness of the range of users and opinions.

In gauging opinions about the usefulness of such sites you could ask students to find articles and news of new developments for themselves. Reporting back to the group again gives the students ownership of the subject and it is a painless way of sharing the collection of a good range of material. Here is one snippet that I found.

> If you can't stand facebook, myspace or any of the other social networking sites where people strive to show how great their lives are, brace yourself for an exercise in one-upmanship that puts them all in the shade. Diddit is the latest import from the US. Tipped as the next online craze, the website exists to allow boasting about things its users claim to have done and plan to do – from top ski resorts visited to marathons run.
>
> Users compile lists of completed experiences, called diddits, and things they plan to do, called wannados, and share them with friends. Achievements are arranged in categories such as travel, sports, and arts and culture. The more lists ticked off the more credits members gather. More than 750,000 diddits have already been completed, and for the particularly egocentric, the site has sections for users to 'share stories of life experiences'. Unkind non-users have suggested this translates as boasting.
>
> > 'With Diddit, we are creating a single place for users to visit for all their diverse experiences in life where they can discover interests they never thought possible, share stories about their activities and engage with dynamic communities', said Paul Gauthier, co-founder of Ludic Labs, the company behind the website. 'Our mission at Diddit is to be the Amazon.com for your life, making us the definitive place people visit to discover and attain life experiences.'

This is the sort of article that can stimulate interest and get the group talking about their own perceptions.

Idea seven: the demands and benefits of rapid technological change

There is no homogeneous speech community on the internet. There are no rules about language uses. Whilst terminology is not always in place, a broad understanding is widespread by users. This is an evolving medium which truly demonstrates the way in which language changes; driven by the general mass of users. Some conventions become accepted and move into general use. Some fall by the wayside. The technology is encouraging us to read, write, speak and listen in different ways. The demands upon the users of language have broadened.

Diverse and highly professional appearing texts can be generated. Access to information has opened up immeasurably. The sense that information is attainable instantly is prevalent.

You could ask your students to create a learning resource in 30 minutes flat that is as impressive looking as possible. Once they have produced their resource, you can investigate the idea of 'impressive'. What is it that they consider to be impressive in their text? The answers to this question will give your group a sense of what they value in a technology-generated text.

Potential exam questions in this area ask for, for example, a 'sensitive understanding of a range of issues and concepts', and a 'conceptualised discussion of ideas surrounding the topic' and to include, 'integrated examples from study which illuminate data and discussion'. The ideas presented here will certainly make for good preparation towards these competences and range of knowledge.

Chapter 6

Original writing

This part of the course allows your students to demonstrate their abilities to produce new texts. The idea is that they create written or spoken pieces that meet the demands of differing audiences and purposes and take into account the conventions of genres and forms.

This should be what I will call 'real writing'. By this I mean that there should be both a real audience for the writing that they produce and that there is a real purpose in writing to that defined audience. A good gauge is whether the writing or speech could be potentially published or performed.

Pre-teaching thinking

The choice of task should come from your students. This choice needs to be motivated by the real interests of the student. Class teaching of genres of writing forms can be helpful as a starting point but can be restrictive in the extreme if students are not allowed to branch out and away from your original model. The student who is writing about something in which they have little interest is going to produce dull writing; the lack of interest is almost always reflected in the writing itself.

A great deal of the investigative work that you have tried in the course to this point has involved examining genre, audience and purpose of printed and spoken texts, and the language features of those texts. All that will be useful now. Students have the opportunity to apply their knowledge of how texts have been created in making their own language choices to complete their original writing. Most syllabuses require that the original pieces be accompanied by a short commentary in which the student reflects upon the needs of their chosen genre and the language decisions that they have taken.

Students need to see the act of writing as being more than the exercises in writing that they have tended to do at GCSE. There, the original writing component to coursework was little more than writing for its own sake; a test of the writer's ability to write functionally. Here, we are moving on to consider how real, purposeful writing is constructed to have the maximum intended impact.

I think that it might be helpful here to give you an example of a successful piece of original writing and to track through the stages of development.

An example: writing for print media

A student of mine had a keen interest in the rock band, Nirvana. He was especially intrigued by the issues thrown up by the publication of the lead singer's, Kurt Cobain, journals. As the journals were found after the singer's death, there was a debate in the press about the ethics of publishing someone's private notebook without that person's permission. My student was interested in writing an article that discussed the issues further. At the outset, he did not really have a fully formulated opinion about whether he was in favour of the publication of Cobain's journal or not.

The student researched the journal and its publication so that he felt informed about the content of the writing. He also looked into identifying an appropriate newspaper or magazine that might have an interested audience and that might potentially publish his writing. This kind of preparation encourages your student to look past what they want to say to who might actually want to hear about it.

Settling on *The Guardian*'s Saturday Review section, he worked his way through several articles featured there, considering the language features that he found. Some linguistic features were internal to the text; visible on the page. By making use of a Fry Graph he was able to consider sentence length and word complexity, determining a reader age for the Review section. After producing a draft of his own writing for *The Guardian*, he would be able to check the reader age of his piece to see if it was approximate to the ones he had analysed.

External features of the text were also examined; what is the voice adopted in the article, what is/are the relationships established between reader and writer, what ideological stance is taken? Detailed analysis of existing published material is important in establishing a successful use of genre for your student's own writing; lots of 'weaker' students may concentrate on the content of the writing that they are to produce. Clearly, those students need to be steered towards thinking about the linguistic 'make-up' of their intended writing. This is, for me, the true role that you should be fulfilling with this module. Your guidance and suggestions will help keep students appropriately focused.

Drafting and revising are clearly very important. My student produced an article of some 1800 words in length, which seemed to fit the kind of requirements his particular module needed. Having consulted me, he went on to look for cohesion in his article: did he have a clear line of enquiry?; Was the article purposeful?; Did the article move towards a conclusive point?

Once he was content with a first draft ready to show to an editor, he emailed *The Guardian* in the hope of receiving feedback on his article. Sometimes, when approaching magazines, newspapers, publishers and the like, no reply is forthcoming. Students should always be encouraged to seek professional opinions about their writing. If you don't ask, you don't get! On this occasion, my student did receive a reply. That reply was largely very favourable although a number of issues were raised. Interestingly, one particular set of ideas that the editor put forward really made an impression upon my student. The editor made/suggested a number of cuts to the article. Large sections were removed and some of the wordings were changed. It was interesting to note how my student felt really rather precious about his writing and did not like the idea that someone other than himself might make changes. This does, of course, demonstrate real commitment to the writing from the student but it is also a lesson learnt.

The editor also chose to remove the word 'shit' from the voice of the piece, indicating that *The Guardian* has a policy of not using/printing taboo language unless it is a direct quotation. Again, my student wanted to discuss this with me at length. He felt that the word was perfect for what he wanted to say and that the choice was surely his, not theirs. This, of course, was true in this instance but he again learnt something about the publishing process.

Because of his genuine interest, he produced an excellent piece of writing; it was directed at an appropriate audience, had real vigour and engagement in the writing and he added to the debate about publishing and ethics. The success of the finished piece lay in the thoroughness of analytical research and the care taken over a subject that had really motivated the student. You can well imagine the genuine level of insight that my student was able to demonstrate in his commentary that detailed the process of learning that he had gone through. Feeling satisfied that he had achieved his ambition to write a piece aimed at the readership of *The Guardian* with the specific purpose of writing informatively, my student was able to move on to find a new audience and new purpose for his second piece, having reserved plenty of word count so that he had enough to fulfil the needs of the word-count limit.

The role that you play here, as teacher, is one of facilitator. You will, from time to time, be called upon to guide students to the next step or push them towards the right path. You will certainly have to be clear about the timeframe in which students are working. Smaller internal deadlines might also be helpful in making sure that students don't just do all the work as the deadline approaches. However, you also need to let the students do this research themselves.

A further example: promotional literature

One of my students was a keen member of a local tennis club. The club coach had noticed falling numbers of attendees of the Saturday sessions for kids. He wanted to get into the local primary schools to speak to children in their assemblies about the club and the opportunities that it offered. He needed some promotional literature that the children could take home afterwards to encourage their parents to take them along to the tennis club. My student quickly saw an opportunity for her to design the leaflets. Here again we see the key ingredients for a potentially successful piece of coursework; a genuine enthusiasm for the subject and a real audience and purpose.

My student went down to the tennis club during the junior coaching session. She took pictures of what was going on and was given JPEGs of the club insignia. She took details of all relevant information that she thought would be needed in the leaflet. She discussed with the tennis coach whether the leaflet was primarily for the parents or the children. This piece of literature afforded an interesting dual audience: the leaflet had to be visually attractive to the children in the first instance and then persuasive and informative for the parents.

My student investigated the various ways that leaflets are laid out. She considered the make-up of the front cover and back cover, the uses of fonts and colours to create impact and even the way that a leaflet should be folded and sized for a primary school child to deliver it home safely. For this piece of coursework we have a clearly-defined set of circumstances with very particular needs linguistically.

Commentary writing

To accompany the finished drafts, a commentary for each piece, documenting the process undergone, needs to be submitted. Different specifications will have varied word limits on this. AQA currently allow 500 words for each commentary. Students should be made aware that the commentary is a real opportunity to demonstrate to their examiner that they are conscious of the significant decisions that they have taken in the process of researching, drafting and evaluating their work.

Commentaries are, of course, tailored toward the individual learning experiences but should broadly discuss the following areas.

- A consideration of the style models that students have looked at and annotated in their research of form, genre and presentational approaches. In the commentary they can discuss what they have learnt from these texts and what they have put into practice based upon this learning.
- Reflections upon actual decisions made during the drafting process. The frameworks should form the basis for this discussion. Students could, for instance, explain their lexical choices within a specific field because of genre or purpose or audience. Perhaps they have had to make use of a Fry Graph to gauge whether their language is accessible for the intended reader.
- Also as part of the assessment of the drafting process, your students should think about changes made to the drafts. Some may have been made because of feedback, either from the intended audience or publisher.
- There should be an evaluation of the final draft. This ought to consider the successes and limitations of the outcome.

Clearly, the commentary is to be completed, or at least written up, after the final draft has been settled upon. Some students may find it useful to log what they are doing and their thinking after each session during the coursework period. These jottings will be really useful and could well form the basis of the commentary.

If time constraints allow, it can be helpful to leave a little time between the production of the finished pieces and the commentaries. This space can lead students to be a little more detached from what they have come up with. This can mean that they are able to read the texts in a detached manner. Hopefully, your student will then be able to see the communication from the point of the receiver rather than producer. In this way they will be able to make more objective judgements about the qualities of the completed final product.

This part of the course is one that should really suit everyone, precisely because they are able to choose the 'content'. At Sixth Form promotion evenings, all those students who are interested in journalism will be keen to hear about this part of the course. Once your course is up and running, here is a real opportunity to demonstrate newly acquired knowledge of frameworks and of the needs of audience, purpose and genre. This unit can illuminate the process of publishing and, most importantly, help students measure their own expectations of what writing and speech might be against the models that they are being presented with.

Chapter 7

Language change

Pre-teaching thinking

Potentially this is an overwhelmingly large subject. It includes the history of the English language (450AD to the present), the technical ways in which languages change, a look at contemporary changes in language and a consideration of English as a world language. It might seem overwhelming but it is also absolutely fascinating.

The assessment of this area is, fortunately, much narrower in scope. Students are given a text, or texts, which illustrate language development. They are invited to comment on what that text shows us about language at that time and the ways that it has developed subsequently.

Deciding what to include and the scope of your study is key to being successful in this unit. Students need to feel that they are prepared as they go into the examination. When the subject-matter appears so vast, students must have the interpretative skills required to look at any text, from any time and any social background. As with language acquisition, you have choices in the approach that you take.

One option is to investigate the history of the English language chronologically. This is helpful to those students who like shape and order to their studies. An overview of the three main periods of the history of English and the significant features of each period makes a good starting point in building that background awareness of what sort of features to look for at certain dates through time. The texts used in examinations are exclusively from the modern period. However, it is important that students know where the language has travelled from to reach this point.

A second option is to consider individual texts in isolation, making the chain of development by linking those texts together. You need not necessarily look at these texts in chronological order. In the examination, your students need to look at the text in front of them and identify how that language is different from today. This skill can be developed quickly through this approach. Students need to be able to spot the internal features of a text (visible features in the text, such as unfamiliar letters or points of grammar) and the external features (the ideologies expressed in the text, the things that the text has to tell us about the time, place and context). Remember that a text from a certain time is not representative of all texts from that time. It is merely one example of a text and needs to be dealt with for what it is, in isolation.

Making a start

One introductory approach, that perhaps mixes the two options above, is to give each of your students a text to research. They then give a presentation to the rest of the group. You can then use their talk as the way into considering the linguistic features of their text. Here is an example of a text that might prove useful in this sort of activity.

In 1589, George Puttenham, the author of the rhetoric manual *The Arte of English Poesie* wrote that:

> Ye shall therefore take the usuall speech of the Court, and that of London and the shires lying about London within lx myles, and not much above. I say not this but that in every shyre of England there be gentlemen and others that speake but specially write as good Southerne as we of Middlesex or Surrey do, but not the common people of every shire to whom the gentlemen, and also the learned clarkes, do for the most part condescend.

After your student has told the group about George Puttenham and the writing that he did and his place in public life and the times that he lived through, you can focus attention on the linguistic features of the language. The starting point for students is always to think how this text differs from their expectations of language.

Internal features

*   *'Usuall'* has a double *'ll'*. Consider why this has dropped to a single 'l'. There are two significant answers here. First, the guiding principle that language has a 'natural' instinctive drive towards being easier to articulate. Language users collectively make their language suit their needs. Note the way that American English today is dropping some written representations of vowel sounds from borrowings, notably 'color' for 'colour'. Secondly, the Chancery, an office responsible for producing documents involved in the running of the country, developed a standard written English so that documents could be read throughout Britain. Patterns of language were established, one of which involved the regularisation of such features as double and single 'l' formations.
*   *'Shyre/shire'*. In this text, which is being rather snooty about the use of language, your students will undoubtedly notice that the word 'shire' has been spelt in two different ways. Again, make your students think this through. The idea that at one time there was no notion of a standard spelling system can be hard for students to grasp. They have, after all, been educated to think that there are right and wrong ways to spell words. It is clear from the subject of this text that at the time there was a debate about 'correctness' in language, an attempt to quantify and shape English. However, the first dictionary, Robert Cawdrey's *The Table Alphabeticall* does not appear until 1604, some 15 years later.
*   *The residual 'e'*. The words 'clarke', 'speake', 'Southerne' and 'Arte' all have an 'e' on the end that is no longer there. Where had it come from? Why did it go? It is a leftover from the case system of Old English, the original grammatical ordering. The function of a word in a sentence was indicated by the way that it was spelt rather than its positioning in the sentence. This led to a word being spelt in a number of ways. Often the ending 'e' would be attached. When this case system was gradually replaced with sentences organised by word order, not all of the endings 'dropped off' immediately. Remember that the debate about standardisation is in its infancy here.

- The word *'condescend'* has undergone some semantic shift. It is perhaps used here in a positive way. The word has taken on a more negative aspect today. The technical term for when a word takes on a more negative shade of meaning is pejoration.

There are a number of other features that could be drawn out here, such as the spelling of 'myles' or the lengthy sentences organised into a sequence of clauses. You will notice that in commenting about a feature of the text it is important to inform this 'feature spotting' with background knowledge about why these features are there.

External features

What I am calling the external features are the ideas, social viewpoints and ideologies contained within the text. The text comes from a time and a place, based upon contemporary wisdom. It demonstrates how language was used and also, in this case, how language was viewed.

- the very fact that Puttenham is writing a rhetoric manual indicates that the debate about the need for a standard is in full swing.
- the idea of 'good Southerne' as a prestige 'voice' may well strike a chord with your students. Puttenham instructs us that the way to speak is demonstrated within a 60-mile radius of London. This value judgement may seem a very prophetic statement from Puttenham. This status has certainly lasted.
- the text is laden with class distinctions. The 'Court', 'gentlemen', 'learned clarkes' and the 'common people' are a clear social hierarchy.
- Puttenham is making a distinction here between written and spoken English. He feels that most are able to write 'good' English throughout the land. When it comes to speech, however, most of the country is 'failing' in its ability to be articulate.
- What does the word 'usuall' indicate here about the ways in which people employed language in the Court? Was there some debate about the way to speak in the Court? Was the way that people at Court were speaking changing? Does the word have a sense of authority, 'usuall' meaning official? Does it carry the sense of, and is an early expression of the idea of, standard? Perhaps the word 'usuall' has undergone some semantic shift. We may not be able to fully answer any of these questions. You need to train your students to be tentative in judgement-making. It is good to acknowledge the limits of what we can discern from texts.

Again, I feel that this investigative approach is most satisfactory in preparing students to meet unseen texts. The text must be viewed as an individual artefact from a time and a place. Here is another text to use in an investigative approach.

William I had invaded a year earlier and is appealing to the people of London in their native tongue, trying to allay their fears about potential changes under the new regime. Again, your students should be trained to consider the internal and external features. As I word-processed the passage I noticed that the grammar and spellcheck had underlined all but four words as being mispellings and 'God' has been highlighted as being grammatically incorrect! Plenty of features then to spot on the page.

In 1067, William I issued the following writ to the citizens of London. The language is English – an uncommon usage in an era when official documents had long been, and for over a century would continue to be, in Latin.

Willm kyng gret Willm bisceop and gosfregd portirefan and ealle pa burhwaru binnan londone frencisce and englisce freondlice. And ic kyde eow paet ic wylle paet get beon eallre paera laga weorde pe gyt waeran on eadwerdes daege kynges. And ic wylle paet aelc cyld beo his faeder yrfnume aefter his faeder daege. And ic nelle gepolian paetaenig wrang beode. God eow gehealde.

Translation: King William greets Bishop William and Port-Reeve Geoffrey and all the burgesses within London, French and English, in a friendly way. And I make known to you that I wish you to enjoy all the rights that you formerly had in the time of King Edward. And I want every child to be the heir of his father after his father's lifetime. And I will not permit any man to do you any wrong. God preserve you.

Outline the significant language features of written English at this time demonstrated in this text and consider how language has developed over time.

1067 is towards the end of the Old English period. The text above is consciously written in English because of its purpose. Over the following few generations the influence of the ruling French classes in Britain was to have a significant effect upon the English language.

Etymology homework

A useful homework for students would be to trace the roots of a word. Following the development of a word from its first recorded instance in the language can give students a 'feel' for how living languages shift to suit the needs of the people that are speaking it.

Consider the word 'crack'.

The word comes from the Gaelic 'craic', meaning conversation. This original meaning, that predates Old English, can be seen in its original sense today in the colloquial expression, "What's the crack?"

As a word, crack has a number of applications.

- Scottish and Irish speakers of English have used the word to mean news, gossip and jokes
- a 'crack regiment' in the sense of expert
- a 'cracking meal' meaning tasty or good
- a 'cracker' – festive game or slang term for an attractive person
- to 'crack on' – to tell a lie or to make progress
- to 'crack one' – to break wind
- to be 'cracked' or to 'crack up'
- crack – the noise
- to 'crack an egg' – to break
- a pejorative noun relating to the female anatomy!

To save you time in choosing words for students to research, there follows a list of words that derived from different sources and whose usages have shifted and changed. This makes these words helpful in studying the nature of change.

Skill – Old Norse
Thing – Old English
Fond – Middle English
Frock – Old French
Pen – Latin
Fee – Old English
Wade – Anglo-Saxon

Clue – Greek
Shambles – Middle English
Girl – Potentially Greek
Villain – Old French
Car – French
Silly – Old English

This list is fairly random and does not include words derived from more recent influences. Where does the word 'window' come from? You'll have to look it up!

What follows next is a suggested selection of texts that students might research at home and then consider collectively in lesson time. I have annotated the list to indicate what each text is usefully indicating about the development of the English language. There are, obviously, plenty of other texts that you can use as points of reference in developing the understanding that your students need to feel empowered to consider the unseen text(s) in the examination.

A slightly different approach to this activity would be to allocate each student a particular year or period for which they then had to find their own text. This encourages the independence of thought required for an investigative approach. Students can make individual seminar presentations to the group. You are also preparing students for the type of research and presentation work that they are likely to encounter at university.

Old English Period 450 – 1150AD

Beowulf is the first great epic poem in the English language. It is tale of a great warrior who protects the Danish king from the monster, Grendel. Linguistically it is useful in providing source material for looking at the nature of Old English.

Ða him Hroþgar gewat   mid his hæleþa gedryht,
eodur Scyldinga,   ut of healle;
wolde wigfruma   Wealhþeo secan,

665
cwen to gebeddan.   Hæfde kyningwuldor
Grendle togeanes,   swa guman gefrungon,
seleweard aseted;   sundornytte beheold
ymb aldor Dena,   eotonweard abead.
Huru Geata leod   georne truwode

670
modgan mægnes,   metodes hyldo.
ða he him of dyde   isernbyrnan,
helm of hafelan,   sealde his hyrsted sweord,

irena cyst,   ombihtþegne,
ond gehealdan het   hildegeatwe.

675

Gespræc þa se goda   gylpworda sum,
Beowulf Geata,   ær he on bed stige:
"No [ok there?] ic me an herewæsmun   hnagran talige,
guþgeweorca,   þonne Grendel hine;
forþan ic hine sweorde   swebban nelle,

680

aldre beneotan,   þeah ic eal mæge.
Nat he þara goda   þæt he me ongean slea,
rand geheawe,   þeah ðe he rof sie
niþgeweorca;   ac wit on niht sculon
secge ofersittan,   gif he gesecean dear".

The Lord's Prayer, Old English version. A further primary source example of our language before 1150AD.

Faeder ure þu þe eart on heofunum,
Si þin nama gehalgod.
To becume þin rice.
Gewurþe ðin willa on eordan swa swa on heofonum.
Urne gedaeghwamlican half syle us todaeg.
And forgyf us ure gyltas, swa swa we forgyfad urum gyltendum. Ane ne gelaed þu us on costnunge,
Ac alys us of yfele.
Soþlice.

The Exeter Book, a book of riddles in Old English is another resource that would prove useful in considering the make-up of the language.

The Lindisfarne Gospels, exhibited in The British Library in London (along with Beowulf) would be a further good example of a text worthy of investigation.

The first thing that normally strikes students about Old English texts is that they can't read them! This then should be a starting point. What is it about the text that makes it indecipherable?

Eighty-five per cent of the vocabulary of Old English has fallen out of use. Students could examine the words that are familiar to them. What sort of words are they? Do they have anything in common? Are certain words, classes of words, more prevalent than others?

There are some unfamiliar letters of which we no longer make use. Can we find reasons why some letters have fallen out of use over time?

Another observation might be that it has a 'harsh' sound or that it sounds like German. Clearly, we have here a language derived from invading Germanic tribes. To take **Beowulf** as an example, the language is 'muscular', full of fricatives and plosives. It is a real workout for the modern mouth.

The grammatical orders are not always what a modern reader would anticipate. As noted above, word order was not the significant feature in creating the function of words in Old English sentences.

As well as these 'internal' features of the texts of Old English, you could discuss with your group how they feel about having become detached from the origins of their language. I would suggest that most merely feel that it is mildly irritating to not be able to read texts in museums. It perhaps makes the past feel even more distant and strange. You might reflect with your class upon the plight of languages which are becoming extinct, subsumed by bigger languages like English. For example, the last speaker of the language Kasabe, spoken in Cameroon, died in November of 1996 before the language had been documented by linguists (there are many languages in the world that do not have a written form). It would surely be more than 'mildly irritating' if that speaker were a relative of yours and he took with him all of your family history. Languages are the repositories of history, the gateposts to identity and cultural understanding.

Middle English Period 1150 – 1500AD

The Canterbury Tales, Geoffrey Chaucer. Chaucer is an important writer for linguistic study because of the sheer range of voices portrayed in his choice of characters on their pilgrimage to Canterbury from London. Chaucer chose his characters from all walks of life and they bring with them the multiplicity of accents, dialects, high-brow foreign borrowings and earthy Anglo-Saxon vocabulary.

The Lord's Prayer. It can be useful to contrast your Old English version of The Lord's Prayer (above) with a Middle English version. This makes a good introduction to the ways in which the language has moved on between the two general time periods. Students will undoubtedly note that this text is much more accessible. So, you explore why they can now, not only identify the text, but fully understand it.

> Oure fadir that art in heuenys,
> Halewid be thy name.
> Thy kingdom come to,
> Be-thy wille don as in heuene an in erthe.
> Give to us this day oure breed ouer other substaunse, And furgiue to us oure dettouris,
> And leede us not into temptacioun,
> But delyuere us from yuel.
> Amen.

Piers Plowman, William Langland. In a period when the English language had made extensive borrowings from French, Langland's verse is notably lacking in such borrowings. This text deals with the plight of the working classes of the Midlands area and is written in alliterative verse making use of the voice of the peasant classes. For the linguist, this text is a good reminder that each text must be considered on its own merits rather than general notions of what one might expect to see in a text written in 1390.

This period is dominated by the invasion of the Norman French in 1066. English became a second-, or indeed third-class language in its own country behind the French of the ruling classes and the language of learning and religion, Latin. Writing in English all but disappears after the Norman Conquest until around 1200. English became an oral language, not thought fitting for serious and important matters.

The Old English inflectional system fell out of use to be replaced with a structural system based on word order. English borrowed extensively from French and Latin.

Rather than finding native equivalents for foreign words, English developed the habit of adopting the foreign words straight into the language. Tri-lingualism was prevalent in business and other professions and words swapped over from one language to another very easily. The alphabet appears more settled and certainly more recognisable to the modern reader. The influx of foreign borrowings lends the language a 'softer' sound, a sound more familiar to our rhythm and stress pattern of today (which is largely, in conversation – stress, unstress).

Tip for your students when approaching Middle English texts. Always consider who is writing and what they are writing about. If the subject is commerce or the business of the Court or writing from the world of medicine, architecture, education, then the language is likely to be borrowing heavily from foreign languages, thought to be suited for the expression of the important matters in life. For instance, all of the technical terms associated with archery are borrowed from French. Texts that deal with more 'low-brow' subjects, such as agriculture, are less likely to include such 'high' language.

In 1476 William Caxton set up the first printing press in Britain, an important moment in the history of the language. Two significant effects were felt. First, the impetus given towards a standardised language was immense. Caxton decided how spellings were going to be fixed and also how texts were to be punctuated. These decisions were then circulated widely through the 96 texts that he printed before his death. Secondly, the advent of the printing press meant that there were more opportunities for people to write. It is estimated that some 20,000 books were printed in the 150 years following. Clearly, this means that we have much more of an evidence base from which to track the development of the language from this time forward. The story of the English language becomes much more certain from this point on.

The Bible, translated into English by William Tyndale. Tyndale was forced abroad in his attempts to bring the word of God to everybody, from the lowliest plough boy to the King. The Bible in England was written in Latin. The services of the Roman Catholic Church were conducted in Latin. For Tyndale to conceive of giving the common people access to the Bible directly (missing out the authority of the Church) – was heretical. Remarkably, his Bibles had to be smuggled into Britain and, once he had been caught, he was executed (in Antwerp) for his treasons. Tyndale's Bible forms the greater part of the King James Bible of 1611 which was placed in all churches in England as 'official' scripture. Tyndale's achievement in producing such beautiful prose in translation cannot be over-estimated. His language is very influential today. Hundreds of words and phrases that we all use every day can be traced directly to Tyndale.

Figure 9: William Tyndale was put to death for his translation of the Bible

Source: William Tyndale, before being strangled and burned at the stake, cries out, "Lord, open the King of England's eyes", woodcut from *Foxe's Book of Martyrs* (1563).

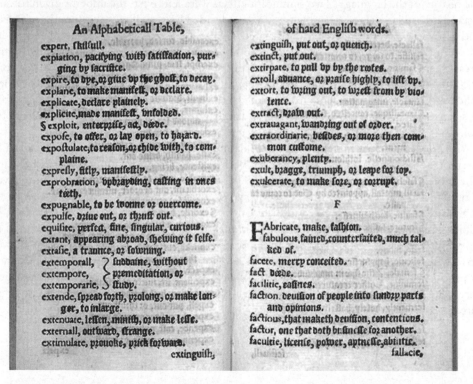

Figure 10: Robert Cawdrey's *A Table Alphabeticall*, published in 1604. This was the first dictionary. Cawdrey chose to list only those words that he deemed 'hard usuall English wordes'.

The First Folio, William Shakespeare, 1623. I think it is probably best to leave you to choose your favourite passages from Shakespeare. There are a number of ways in which Shakespeare's contribution to the English language can be tracked. First, he was the inventor or promoter of new words. Well over 2,000 words that we use today are first recorded in a Shakespeare play. He was also very keen on compounding (putting together two words that had not previously been thought of together, forming a new word and idea), creating many more new forms of expression, and indeed, new ways of thinking. Shakespeare made use of all the new words that abounded at this time as well as the language of the Bible and borrowings from the Latin he used at school. He also brought in regional words from his own accent, Midlands.

Dr Johnson's Dictionary of 1755 has a number of very entertaining definitions within its pages. To look at a page from the dictionary can be an illuminating way of considering the various fates of words that have prospered or died out or shifted in their meanings. Given the quirky nature of some aspects of the dictionary, like the very personal and subjective nature of some definitions, it can also be an interesting resource in considering the development of the genre of the dictionary.

OA'TMEAL. *n. ſ.* [*oat* and *meal.*] Flower made by grinding oats.

 Oatmeal and butter, outwardly applied, dry the ſcab on the head.   *Arbuthnot on Aliment.*

  Our neighbours tell me oft, in joking talk,

  Of aſhes, leather, *oatmeal*, bran, and chalk.   *Gay.*

OA'TMEAL. *n. ſ.* An herb.   *Ainſworth.*

OATS. *n. ſ.* [aten, Saxon.] A grain, which in England is generally given to horſes, but in Scotland ſupports the people.

 It is of the graſs leaved tribe ; the flowers have no petals, and are diſpoſed in a looſe panicle : the grain is eatable. The meal makes tolerable good bread.   *Miller.*

  The *oats* have eaten the horſes.   *Shakeſpeare.*

 It is bare mechaniſm, no otherwiſe produced than the turning of a wild *oatbeard*, by the inſinuation of the particles of moiſture.   *Locke.*

 For your lean cattle, fodder them with barley ſtraw firſt, and the *oat* ſtraw laſt.   *Mortimer's Huſbandry.*

 His horſe's allowance of *oats* and beans, was greater than the journey required.   *Swift.*

OA'TTHISTLE. *n. ſ.* [*oat* and *thiſtle.*] An herb. *Ainſ.*

Figure 11: Dr Johnson's Dictionary (1755)

Whilst the dictionaries are recognised as being in the early modern period, they are significant in ushering in one of the key themes of the modern period, that being standardisation. It is common ground that from 1500 onwards, the language suddenly took off in terms of the sheer size of the vocabulary. This led to the desire to quantify the language. Dictionaries and grammars are symptomatic of this increase in the word horde.

The Modern Period (1500 – the present)

Characterising the development of the English Language through its early periods helps your students to appreciate what had happened to the language before the date of any texts that might be chosen for examination purposes. Texts are chosen exclusively from the Modern period.

A timeline activity to share with your group

Here is an activity that you can try that will help to highlight where understanding is clear and where any gaps exist in the knowledge of your students. It will also have the added benefit of producing a revision resource.

Draw a timeline from 450AD to the present, leaving a little space for the future. Lead a discussion in filling in the significant features of language change over the history of the English language.

Start by dividing the timeline into the three main periods. For each period draw up a list of features that you might expect to spot in a text from that time. For example, in Old English: dialectal vocabulary, 'Germanic sound', lots of fricatives and plosives, inflectional endings that determine the function of words, unfamiliar letters, interchangeable u/v, lots of compound words, a small word hoard in comparison to today, 85% of vocabulary no longer in use, the survival of 'grammatic' words, such as conjunctions and connectives.

Add to this, along the timeline, the names of significant texts and influential figures that you have studied. You should also add-in the various ways in which language has undergone change, for example, colonisation, the classical period of English literature, the invention of the printing press, invasions, the great vowel shift etc.

I have always found that my students have found it easier to internalise this information if they have had a hand in producing the timeline themselves.

In considering the modern period, you are again able to offer the student the opportunity to develop important study skills. Having outlined the two earlier periods, you could entrust the research of important linguistic developments in the modern era to the students.

This process could begin with a group discussion of what they need to know. Open and collaborative questioning can set the guidelines for choosing how and what to research.

Rather than have this timeline tell you about the modern period, get your students to research into the topic. They could try to identify five key events or factors that have helped to shape the language. Groups could present their findings to the class and try to make a case for the particular area that they have researched.

Just in case you are feeling that we are not being all that helpful here, here is a list of 'key' areas that should prove to be illuminating.

- social upheavals of 1640–60
- increases in trade

- British settlement of America
- Inkhorn Debate 1560–1640
- the 1611 King James authorised Bible
- The Renaissance (1500s and 1600s)
- the Great Vowel Shift 1450–1750
- the impact of the British Empire.

Let your students chart their ways through the impact that these and other factors have had upon the language in the modern period. Collectively, they can join the different factors onto the timeline creating a clear sense of chronology.

The exam boards might also choose to make use of a text from the very recent past. These sorts of texts often throw students as they appear not to have changed very much. Certainly, the explicit internal features visible on the page seem to be like those of today. More modern texts need very careful consideration.

An example of a more modern text for study

This is the text printed on a tea towel.

We are Survivors
(For those born before 1940)

We were born before television, before penicillin, polio shots, frozen foods, Xerox, contact lenses, videos and the Pill. We were before radar, credit cards, split atoms, laser beams and ballpoint pens, before dishwashers, tumble driers, electric blankets, air conditioners, drip-dry clothes ... and before man walked on the moon.

We got married first then lived together (how quaint can you be?). We thought 'fast food' was what you ate in Lent, a 'Big Mac' was an oversized raincoat and 'crumpet' we had for tea. We existed before house husbands, computer dating and 'sheltered accommodation' was where you waited for a bus.

We were before daycare centres, group homes and disposable nappies. We never heard of FM radio, tape decks, artificial hearts, word processors, or young men wearing earrings. For us 'time sharing' meant togetherness, a 'chip' was a piece of wood or fried potato, 'hardware' meant nuts and bolts and 'software' wasn't a word.

Before 1940 'Made in Japan' meant junk, the term 'making out' referred to how you did in your exams, 'stud' was something that fastened a collar to a shirt and 'going all the way' meant staying on a double-decker bus to the terminus. In our day, cigarette smoking was 'fashionable', 'grass' was mown, 'coke' was kept in the coalhouse, a 'joint' was a piece of meat you ate on Sundays and 'pot' was something you cooked in. 'Rock Music' was a fond mother's lullaby, 'Eldorado' was an ice cream, a 'gay person' was the life and soul of the party, while 'aids' just meant beauty treatment or help for someone in trouble.

We who were born before 1940 must be a hard bunch when you think of the way in which the world has changed and the adjustments we have had to make. No wonder there is a generation gap today ... BUT

By the grace of God . . . we have survived!

What a fantastic text for language study. The voice makes a direct appeal to a generation for whom the world has produced a dizzying new variety of words. Some of these words are brand new, such as 'software'. However, most are words that were once familiar but the meaning of them has changed as the world looks for language to describe the times; the new experiences that society throws up ('time sharing') and the new inventions that technology brings ('chip').

Whilst the text is fairly lighthearted, you have here a good example of the prescriptivist attitude towards language, a hankering for the language that you grew up with and understood, and that was 'right'.

It is also interesting to note how some of the modern words that are being highlighted here, in the 1990s, as being brash and new-fangled, have, in fact, now dated somewhat. 'Time sharing' is awkward having been replaced with the more versatile expression 'time share'. 'Tape deck' suffers because technology has moved.

There is an underlying sense of moral decay here. The voice feels that standards have slipped. Young men wearing earrings, promiscuity and drug abuse are all illustrated in the way that, for this voice, words have undergone a process of pejoration (the meaning has become more negative).

Some of the words that are highlighted have kept their original sense ('chip', 'hardware', 'joint') but have added new meanings. Perhaps it is the new meaning that is the first thing to come into the minds of people today when they hear these words.

The fact that this is the text of a tea towel that is for sale demonstrates the interest that language has in creating an identity, in this instance for a generation of people. The voice suggests that having come 'before' all of this change lends this generation some sort of permanence or intrinsic value.

The following revision activity is useful in helping your students consider the depth of their knowledge. Actively producing materials that explain what they know to a younger audience will help them to organise and sift through their own understanding. You might also get some resources for Year 9!

Language change revision activity

In order to consolidate what you have already learned about language change, you are going to produce a small package that will help Year 9 students learn about *The History of the English Language*.

The package that you produce should contain:

- Relevant and interesting facts about our changing language;
- Analysis of why language has changed;
- Explanations of some of the effects of language change;
- Some tasks that students can undertake.

This piece of work will help you to become more confident about the extent and depth of your understanding of linguistics. It is designed to give you every opportunity to become certain of the skills you need to succeed in this element of your A2 studies.

In the examination you will have to: *communicate clearly; make use of appropriate terminology; apply and explore frameworks; understand, discuss and explore concepts and issues of language;* and *analyse and evaluate variation in the meanings of spoken and written language.* Here is an opportunity to develop these skills further.

You will need to endeavour to bring to bear all of your skills in writing for different audiences (14-year-old students) and purposes (to educate). You will also need to assimilate the knowledge and information that you already have with new findings that independent research will bring.

Good luck with your research!

The future for English?

By way of introducing your consideration of the way that English is developing and how it might grow in the future, you could try the following activity. You could set it as a homework and use the notes made by each student as the basis of the follow-up discussion in the next lesson.

How will words 'prosper' in the future?

Consider the following words and make brief notes so that you are ready to join in with our discussion about them. The questions that I wish you to ask yourself are as follows;

i.   how will these words 'prosper' in the future?
ii. what factors will effect this?
iii. pick the three that you think will last longest.

Your words are:

- book
- computer
- gramophone
- sputnik
- cool
- [put a name in, perhaps put your own last name!]
- water
- [any other words of your choice, perhaps a very new word would be good].

This activity encourages students to think through factors that create change in a living language. Again, it helps the student to be flexible in their approach to unseen texts.

Language change: wider reading opportunity

Whilst the assessment of this area concentrates on the English language, it can prove helpful to measure English against other languages.

Most obviously, the students can be asked to research into the way that English has developed from common routes with Germanic languages. Students can trace back through families of languages.

Perhaps as a development of this activity, students could each be allocated languages to see how they compare with English. The growing family of contemporary Englishes would make a good group of 'languages' for investigation. To consider the subtleties between British English against the English spoken in places like South Africa, Singapore, India and North America should prove illuminating. You might be able to open a discussion about whether English is fragmenting into a family of languages in the modern world. Students might be encouraged to ask themselves what are the possible ends to this process.

Another way in which it is possible to examine English is to trace the development of other modern languages. Here is the example of French. In researching French I noticed that it belongs to a different family of languages, the Romance languages which includes Italian, Spanish, Portuguese and Rumanian. However, I was struck by a number of similarities that exist. These similarities might open up a different line of enquiry about the ways in which languages share common means of developing.

Two thematic sequences of developing genres

This next section of the language change focus is a series of texts, two from specific genres. The specific themed texts that we have chosen are recipes and autobiography. They cover the modern time-period of the development of the English language. Clearly, you could also develop your own series based on the pattern exemplified here, to suit your own students' interests.

As briefly mentioned in the *Pre-teaching thinking* section for *Language Change*, it is important that students do not come to see texts as representative of all texts from that time. In exams, students can often make this mistake. A general awareness of where the language was up to, in any given period that you have been working on, needs to be informing the students' reading of the particular text in front of them. They need to consider the text for what it is in terms of the writer, reader, context and genre.

One way of teaching this insight and approach is to create a thematic sequence of texts that share a common factor. Here we offer you the format of recipes and, secondly, the idea of 'home' as expressed through autobiographical writings. These are just choices that we have made to demonstrate range. Your students may, for instance, need to see that genres have developed over time. They may assume that writing for particular audiences has remained fixed. You can develop your own sequences that meet the needs of your own students. Indeed, your students could build their own resource bank for analysis to encompass their own particular interests. *Remember that the content of the pieces chosen is not as important as the process of exploring that the students will undertake.*

In approaching a sequence of texts, students should have in mind the linguistic frameworks that you have encouraged them to employ throughout the course. If a student is stumped by a text they can go back to grammar, semantics, phonology, etc. Language study is about observing, measuring, sifting and recording the features demonstrated and seeking to understand the motives of the writer or speaker at the time. Careful observation of how things were can then be compared with current expectations of a similar text in today's world. How does it differ? What factors have changed the genre or value of the text?

As a teacher, are you able to resist the desire to tell your students how things are/were? I know that there is a great temptation to be a font of wisdom. To point out 'know-able' things feels like the job of the teacher. However, the student needs to develop the skill of analysing texts and will become more proficient at this skill if they are allowed to pursue it for themselves. I think that your role here is to guide, nudging gently, towards the interesting areas of linguistic research.

Recipes

Hannah Glasse, The Art Of Cookery made Plain and Easy (1747)

Let's begin our trawl through the language of cookery in 1747 with Hannah Glasse's recipe for making pastry for sweet and savoury dishes. These recipes are from her bestseller, *The Art Of Cookery made Plain and Easy*. The audience for the book, as explained by the author herself in the Preface, were 'the lower sort'. What she meant by this was that here was a book of instruction for the servants. This sort of book was fashionable in the 1700s.

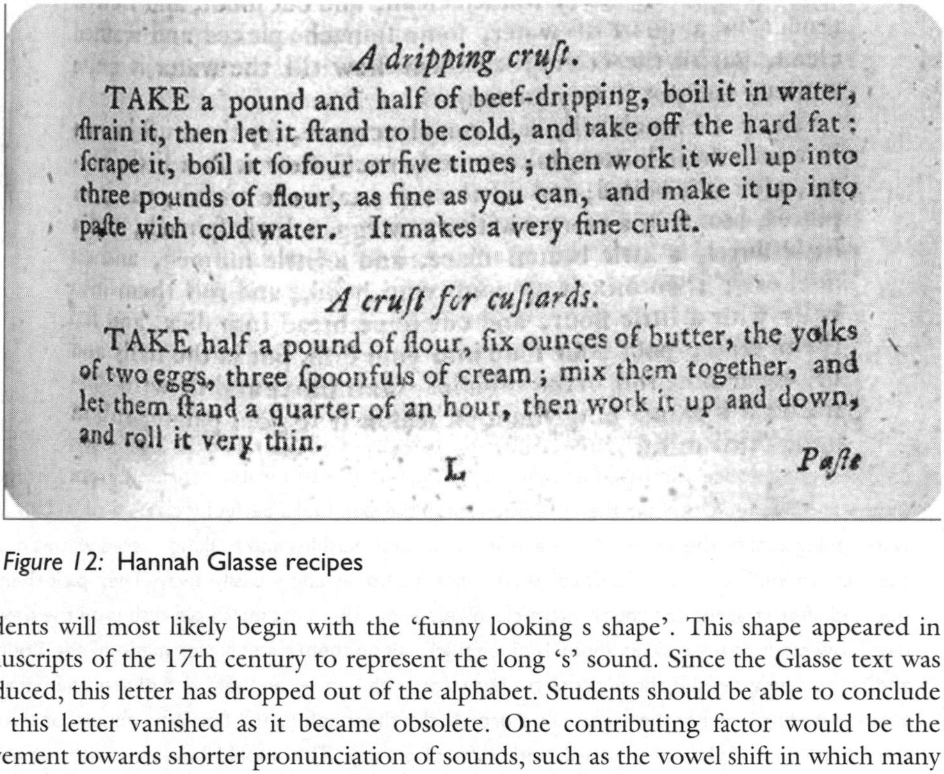

A dripping cruft.

TAKE a pound and half of beef-dripping, boil it in water, ftrain it, then let it ftand to be cold, and take off the hard fat : fcrape it, boil it fo four or five times ; then work it well up into three pounds of flour, as fine as you can, and make it up into pafte with cold water. It makes a very fine cruft.

A cruft for cuftards.

TAKE half a pound of flour, fix ounces of butter, the yolks of two eggs, three fpoonfuls of cream ; mix them together, and let them ftand a quarter of an hour, then work it up and down, and roll it very thin.

L   *Pafte*

Figure 12: Hannah Glasse recipes

Students will most likely begin with the 'funny looking s shape'. This shape appeared in manuscripts of the 17th century to represent the long 's' sound. Since the Glasse text was produced, this letter has dropped out of the alphabet. Students should be able to conclude that this letter vanished as it became obsolete. One contributing factor would be the movement towards shorter pronunciation of sounds, such as the vowel shift in which many long vowels contracted.

The first word 'TAKE' is capitalised and the word 'Paste' appears at the bottom right hand corner of the page. These are accepted discourse features of the time. The capitalisation of the first word of a block of text indicates the beginning of a new section. Perhaps this is legacy from the days of illuminated texts. The first word that appears on the following page is printed at the bottom of the page, in this instance 'paste'.

There are some lexical items that stand out as being worthy of discussion; 'boil it so', 'well up' and 'make it up'. Each expression is unfamiliar; semantic shift has taken place.

When the Norman French arrived in 1066 and occupied the privileged positions of society in England, many French loanwords made their way into the English language. Often these words described the finer things in life, such as the art of cookery. It is interesting to note here that the technical words 'strain', 'boil', 'roll' and 'ounce' are all borrowed from Old French. The names for the foodstuffs are also Old French – beef, cream, butter and custard. Interestingly, the words 'crust' and 'custard' have the same root word, the Old French word *crouste*. 'Scrape' is from Old Norse.

The general grammatical structure of the text (long multi-clause sentencing) suits the form of a set of instructions. The language is straightforward and functional, which in turn suits the 'lower sort' audience.

Here, there is a sense of authority, the idea that this is the right way to cook. Cooking itself is presented as functional; a necessity. In the 20th century, the form of recipe book has evolved to encompass the idea that cookery is part of lifestyle choices and also that there is an element of aesthetics that is not present in Hannah Glasse's writing.

Mrs Beeton, Book of Household Management (1861)

Mrs Beeton's *Book of Household Management*, published 114 years after Hannah Glasse's recipe is a further example of how texts about cookery were aimed at instructing the working class in methods of cooking. It is worth noting that the text has become more elaborately detailed and has a more extensive range of 'lessons' for its reader. Mrs Beeton has extended the function of her text from being a description of how to cook to a full account of how to run all aspects of a kitchen.

FRICASSEED CALF'S FEET

861. INGREDIENTS—A set of calf's feet; for the batter allow for each egg 1 tablespoonful of flour, 1 tablespoonful of bread crumbs, hot lard or clarified dripping, pepper and salt to taste.

Mode—If the feet are purchased uncleaned, dip them into warm water repeatedly, and scrape off the hair, first one foot and then the other, until the skin looks perfectly clean, a saucepan of water being kept by the fire until they are finished. After washing and soaking in cold water, boil them in just sufficient water to cover them, until the bones come easily away. Then pick them out, and after straining the liquor into a clean vessel, put the meat into a pie-dish until the next day. Now cut it down in slices about 1/2 inch thick, lay on them a stiff batter made of egg, flour, and bread crumbs in the above proportion; season with pepper and salt, and plunge them into a pan of boiling lard. Fry the slices a nice brown, dry them before the fire for a minute or two, dish them on a napkin, and garnish with tufts of parsley. This should be eaten with melted butter, mustard, and vinegar. Be careful to have the lard boiling to set the batter, or the pieces of feet will run about the pan. The liquor they were boiled in should be saved, and will be found useful for enriching gravies, making jellies, &e. &e.

Time—About 3 hours to stew the feet, 10 or 15 minutes to fry them.

Average cost, in full season, 9d. each.

Sufficient for 8 persons.

Seasonable from March to October.

Note.—This dish can be highly recommended to delicate persons.

Cookery in 1861 was a very different experience to cookery in 1747; the methods of preparation are more sophisticated and the style of the dish is elevated by offering serving suggestions at the end of the recipe. It is very functional language and this relationship between text and context is an ideal starting point for discussion.

Attitudes to food and its preparation were different in 1861. The first sentence describes a process that would now be undertaken by a butcher or in a factory; the phrase 'scrape off the hair' shows a far more physical process. The skills that are required of domestic staff are extensive and from the time taken to prepare 'fricasseed calf's feet' also clearly indicate that this is a text aimed at domestic staff who will be preparing the meal for their employers and guests.

There are many interesting internal features in the text too. The structure of the text is entirely as we would expect. Its discourse is sequential as shown by the opening words of sentences: 'after', 'then' and 'now'. The use of declarative sentences throughout indicates the writer's authority and therefore gives the reader some confidence. The text relies on explicit semantics throughout to ensure that the instructions are easily followed: 'until the skin looks perfectly clean', 'put the meat into a pie dish' and 'dry them before the fire'. There are changes in expression that mark this text as very different from later recipes. Marking the shift in expression from Glasse to Beeton is fulfilling. Examples of phrases worthy of study are 'lay on them a stiff batter' and 'run about the pan'. These expressions now seem antiquated and it is difficult to imagine a world where a writer fails to realise the humorous connotations of disembodied calf's feet running around in boiling lard.

Mrs Beeton's recipe illustrates the movement from writing that is simply aimed at a 'lower sort' to writing that appeals to an increasingly well-educated class of skilled servants. It also demonstrates how increasingly exotic names for dishes are entering the language and how the language of cookery, already full of borrowings from French, is now embracing new loan words.

Jean Rey, The Whole Art of Dining (1921)

Moving forward 60 years to 1921, we come to *The Whole Art of Dining* by Jean Rey. In the following extract, Rey discusses a lack of sophistication in the eating habits of the working classes.

THE WORKING CLASS TEA

The tea of the English working class is the most eccentric of meals, and one of the greatest injuries a gourmet could possibly conceive (according to the ideas of Brillat-Savarin); for with the tea they partake of various kinds of salted meat and dried fish, such as "corned-beef," kippers, bloaters, red herrings, winkles, shrimps, pickles, watercresses, cucumber, lettuce, jam or marmalade, bread and butter, and cake. This incongruous kind of food may, no doubt, be quite nice and tasty for this class of people, but it must shock any one endowed with refined epicurean instinct.

The idea of cooking as art form drives this book. It is aimed at a society of leisured, wealthy sophisticates, eating in lavish dining halls and enjoying decadent picnics. In this extract, the efforts of the working class to feed themselves are mocked; mocked because of a lack of refinement.

Characterised here is a world that is strictly divided into a social hierarchy. I am sure that there is no real consciously intended malice towards the writer's perception of the working class. This simply is his world order. Admittedly, it is most certainly a world order that is much under threat in the aftermath of the First World War. Perhaps Rey's book is partly a reaction to the devastation of Europe, and the sense of a much-needed 'normality' being linked with a 'right way' to eat, a predictable response.

I can hear the language of war echoing through the text. The food is described as 'one of the greatest injuries' and 'a shock'. The selection of food is 'incongruous', lacking shape and order. There is a clear sense of *us* and *them* in this writing.

Notice the use of divergent language (distancing your voice from your subject) in expressions like '… they partake of …' and '… any one endowed with …' used in conjunction with convergent overtones (borrowing from the sociolect of your subject) in the expression '… quite nice and tasty …'.

Elizabeth David, French Provincial Cooking (1960)

When Elizabeth David published *French Provincial Cooking* in 1960 she was already an established writer on European tastes and recipes. Her books are written from her experiences and have the tone of an anthropologist exploring culture through food as much as they are instructional manuals. She is writing for an audience more representative of the general public than Rey's but one that still has some privilege socially and educationally.

MOULES À LA NORMANDE

MUSSELS WITH CREAM SAUCE

A grander version of *moules marinière*.

Melt I oz. of butter in a wide pan, add a shallot, parsley and a few celery leaves all coarsely chopped, then a large glass of dry cider or dry white wine. Add 3 quarts of cleaned mussels, cover the pan for the first few minutes, then remove the lid and take out the mussels as they open and transfer them to a warmed dish or tureen. Strain the remaining stock through muslin, return it to the pan and let it reduce by about half. Put about 1/3 pint of double cream to boil in a small pan, so that it reduces and thickens, and meantime remove the empty half shells from the cooked mussels.

Add the boiling cream to the mussel stock, and off the fire stir in a good lump of butter. Pour bubbling hot over the mussels, add chopped parsley and serve quickly. For four people. One of the best wines to drink with mussels is a fresh clean Muscatel from the Loire.

Elizabeth David writes for an audience that will be cooking the recipes for themselves, for friends or family. This recipe follows the introduction to cooking mussels where David explains 'The Cleaning and Cooking of Mussels'. The expectations of the everyday cook in

1960s Britain have been raised and cooking with cider or wine and fresh herbs is becoming a familiar sight. The semantic field here is of fresh, healthy and coastal food. 'Shallot', 'parsley' and 'celery leaves' are indicative of a lifestyle which is embracing previously exotic tastes. 'Mussels' themselves have been transformed from pickled seafood sold in seaside towns and pubs on Friday nights to easy-to-cook, everyday food. David's travels have enabled her to introduce a new lifestyle to her homeland.

The grammar is typical and predictable, all future tense, sentences begin with verbs, 'melt', 'add', and 'strain'. David's adherence to conventions place her firmly in the tradition of cookery writing and she, like Beeton before her, offers the reader personal recommendations. Though still a declarative sentence, her final one does soften the tone of the recipe slightly as it is tempered by the phrase 'one of the best'; her readers are reassured by the recommendation and trusted to make their own choice.

It is this relationship between writer and reader that is most notable about the discourse here. David is a guide, an expert one, but a guide all the same. She has softened the didactic tone of Beeton and Rey's texts and has begun to trust in the judgement of her readers.

Culturally David is very easy to place in a society where gender liberation and class equality were driving forces of social reform. She writes to an audience able and willing to travel further afield for their holidays. Student populations were radicalised and were driving changes from the restricted and restrictive culture of the 1950s. Elizabeth David paved the way for cookery to become the cultural phenomenon that it is today.

Keith Floyd, *Floyd on France* (1987)

This recipe is from *Floyd on France* published in 1987. It was accompanied by a television programme of the same name. Keith Floyd was one of the first chefs of the modern period in Britain to add an element of 'personality' to the presentation of recipes. The idea of cookbooks was moving towards having an element of lifestyle attached to it, in a more inclusive way than the rather snotty and condescending voices of the past.

However, Floyd does still display an element of snobbery in his disgust for the ways in which landlords and restauranteurs have produced a version of a very popular recipe of the time. 'Raped and pillaged' is used here for comedic effect, demonstrating Floyd's outrage. Taboo language is indicative of his approach.

In 1987 France was seen as a sophisticated place and its cuisine considered high culture. Visiting France was a pursuit of the middle classes. Floyd makes play of the idea of authenticity in his recipe. It is not imitation like the pub and restaurant copies that so upset him. He speaks with authority about the need to stick to the recipe. Floyd relies upon his strident personality; a personality that readers will have seen for themselves from watching the television programme.

A new feature of the genre of cookery books is also exemplified here – photographic illustrations. This advancement in the investment in a new presentational feature also increased the move towards these kinds of books being about leisure and refinement. The cookery book that followed often appeared as large hardback books meant to be left about on coffee tables; they were suggestive of style.

Floyd speaks much of the time as an equal with his reader and offers advice past that of ingredients and timings.

BEEF BOURGIGNON

This splendid stew has been raped and pillaged by pub and winebar cooks the length and breadth of this fair land of ours – they add peppers and other unmentionable ingredients to what must be a simple, slow-cooked dish with no deviation from this recipe.

Serves 6 – 8

3lb (1.5 kg) well-hung beef shin, shoulder and

neck, cut in bitesize chunks

5 onions, roughly chopped

5 carrots, roughly chopped

5 shallots, roughly chopped

3 cloves garlic, chopped

6 sprigs thyme

2 bay leaves

1 handful parsley, roughly chopped

2 bottles red Burgundy

6 thick slices streaky bacon, cubed

1 large brandy

5 fl oz (150ml) Madeira

1 small calf's foot (optional, but preferable!)

8 oz (250g) mushrooms, finely chopped

butter

7 oz (200g) baby onions, peeled

salt and pepper

Marinate the beef, onions, carrots, shallots, garlic and herbs in the wine overnight. Remove the meat and reserve the marinade.

In a large heavy-bottomed saucepan, fry the bacon and then add the meat and brown. Add the Madeira and barely cover with the reserved marinade which you have sieved, discarding the vegetables. Add the calf's foot. Cover and simmer on a low flame for three hours. Top up with the marinade if it seems to be drying out.

Fry the mushrooms in a little butter and add to the meat. Toss in the baby onions. When the onions are tender, add the salt and pepper. Serve very hot.

> There is no mystery. Careful shopping, fresh ingredients and an unhurried approach are nearly all you need. There is one more thing – love. With a combination of these things you can become an artist – not perhaps in the representational style of a Dutch Master, but rather more like Gauguin, the naïve, or Van Gogh, the impressionist. Plates or pictures of sunshine taste of happiness and love. This is the philosophy of the French and it is my philosophy.

Nigel Slater, *Appetite* (2000)

Nigel Slater offers his readers a relaxed and informal set of recipes in his book *Appetite* published in 2000. Through the exploration of how to have a relationship with food and cooking that fits comfortably with our modern lifestyles he demonstrates a further shift in cookery writing. He is writing about ways to fit good food in to our lives, rather than offering us a renewed lifestyle through cooking.

> *a solitary and utterly luxurious fish supper*
>
> A deeply delicious and satisfying fish supper. Nevertheless, you will need some bread to mop up the garlicky juice and, as this is not a filling meal, a pudding of some sort to follow.
>
> Enough for 1, with crusty white bread and something to follow
>
> **butter – sweet, pale and unsalted, as always**
>
> **scallops – as many as you fancy, but I suggest about 4 large ones**
>
> **garlic – sweet, juicy and young; a large clove, peeled and chopped**
>
> **parsley – a small palmful or so, chopped but not too finely**
>
> Take a small shallow pan, one that is light enough to pick up and shake, then melt enough butter to cover the bottom thinly. Let it sizzle and froth over a high heat. When the foam subsides and the butter falls silent, lower in the wobbly, glistening scallops and let them cook (they will spit at you) for two to three minutes, until a sticky, golden crust has formed on the underside. Turn them, let them colour underneath, then whip them out on to a warm plate, throw out the browned butter and put in some more, sweet and fresh. Then, as it froths, add the crushed garlic, swirl the pan quickly around, toss in the parsley and tip it all, sweetly frothing, over the scallops. Now eat up.

The first of many striking features that place this as a 21st century text is the description of the meal as a 'solitary supper'. Slater is writing for people who live real lives and not every meal is a dinner party and not everyone wants to spend more than ten minutes making a meal. He also understands that we can indulge ourselves alone rather than only eating the best food when there are guests. His audience is entirely different from previous audiences of cookery writing: they are children of the late 20th century and adults of the 21st.

The informal register of the piece creates the sense that we are listening to him. Phrases such as 'garlicky juice', 'throw out the browned butter' and 'Now eat up' show a familiarity with the reader that closes the distance rather than adhering to the expert and amateur relationship earlier writers establish. This informal relationship translates to the relationship that we can have with food, too: 'swirl', 'toss' and 'whip them out' are more physical verbs, more fun and more sensual than functional instructions like boil or chop. A further feature of his sentences is the adjectival phrases that he allows himself to increase the appeal of his suggestions. 'Wobbly, glistening scallops' is not a phrase that Mrs Beeton would not have written.

The text is so rich beyond these features. You might discuss the descriptions of the ingredients which are suggestive rather than didactic. You could explore the relationships between graphology, grammar and voice, using uncapitalised titles as a starting point. Asking questions about the way that Slater's audience is treated as being special though equal to him at the same time invites consideration of where he sees himself in the history of cookery writers. This text, as we near the end of this section of the book, is thoroughly modern and highlights how language change can be illustrated by texts which, without historical context, can seem 'normal' to today's reader.

Madhur Jaffrey, *Ultimate Curry Bible* (2003)

Madhur Jaffrey's *Ultimate Curry Bible* won The Guild of Food Writers' Cookery Book of the Year Award in 2003. It begins with a 26–page history of the fashion for curry around the world, encompassing India, Singapore, Malaysia, Indonesia, Thailand, South Africa, Kenya, Great Britain, Trinidad, Guyana, Japan and the USA.

When I left India almost forty years ago, my mother gave me three essential kitchen utensils, a grinding stone (sil batta), a brass platter for making dough (paraat) and a cast-iron kadhai. I still have all three, each glistening with years of wear, each inscribed with my name.

Kadhais are used, just like a wok, for deep-frying, stir-frying, steaming and – only in South Asia – for reducing milk to make sweets. In this particular recipe, it is used for stir-frying chicken very quickly and easily to produce an uncommonly delicious dish.

Here is the opening to a recipe for 'Kadhai' Chicken (Karhai Murgh). After this introduction, the recipe follows the by now well-established formula of list of ingredients followed by method.

The extract above demonstrates the truly cosmopolitan and global nature of the outlook of this cookery book. Along with the British taste for curry has come a vocabulary, swallowed whole (sorry) into the English language. Notice the way that Kadhai is placed into the sentence above without any kind of explanation. Note also the valuing of the non-English words for grinding stone and a brass platter. It is part of the world view being expressed here. It is important to the cookery to know where the food has come from and the names of the foodstuffs and utensils.

This text suggests that the foods and cultures are separate but also linked. The writer is saying that the recipe and the culture that it comes from are personal to her but there is a real sense of sharing and, perhaps, of breeding understanding between cultures.

This text strikes me as wholly inclusive. It is about the writer's relationship with the art of cookery. However, there isn't the rather authoritarian air of say Jean Rey or Mrs Beeton. What is being shared here is enthusiasm and knowledge rather than prescription.

These seven texts trace the development of the formula of recipes from 1700 to the present. They can be used as a standalone unit that traces how a genre of writing develops. Of course, there are endless possibilities for you to add to and develop this unit. Your group might become interested in a particular line of enquiry within the genre; you could trace intended audiences through time, attitudes towards food preparation, the formulaic layout of recipes or any number of other smaller focuses.

One benefit of tracing the development of a particular type of writing is that students will appreciate that the texts in the exam are not representative of all texts and writing from that time. They will make use of their linguistic knowledge developed in the first year of the course: intended audience, purpose and context.

In the texts represented here, I think that we see a form of writing that has moved from being formal, instructional and authoritarian to being conversational, advisory and inclusive. This is the journey of the genre, and that is the essence of the assessed activities at A level; how is the text in front of the student in the exam different to their expectation of that type of text today? Measuring that distance, both in terms of internal features on the page and the wider external features that the text indicates, is the task.

AUTOBIOGRAPHY

Mary Seacole, *The Wonderful Adventures of Mrs Seacole in Many Lands* (1857)

Mary Seacole volunteered as a nurse and was involved in frontline action during the Crimean War. Originally from the Caribbean she was refused the opportunity to work in an official capacity as a nurse so she took her own path. As well as providing medical care to the injured and dying, she also traded, offering vital provisions.

> Would you like, gentle reader, to know what other things suggestive of home and its comforts your relatives and friends in the Crimea could obtain from the hostess of Spring Hill? I do not tell you that the following articles were all obtainable at the commencement, but many were. The time was indeed when, had you asked me for mock turtle and venison, you should have had them, preserved in tins, but that was when the Crimea was flooded with plenty – too late, alas! to save many whom want had killed; but had you been doing your best to batter Sebastopol about the ears of the Russians in the spring and summer of the year before last, the firm of Seacole and Day would have been happy to have served you with (I omit ordinary things) linen and hosiery, saddlery, caps, boots and shoes, for the outer man; and for the inner man, meat and soups of every variety in tins (you can scarcely conceive how disgusted we all became at last with preserved provisions); salmon, lobsters, and oysters, also in tins, which last beaten upinto fritters, with onions, butter, eggs, pepper, and salt, were very good; game, wild fowl, vegetables, also preserved, eggs, sardines, curry powder, cigars, tobacco, snuff, cigarette papers,

> tea, coffee, tooth powder, and currant jelly. When cargoes came in from Constantinople, we bought great supplies of potatoes, carrots, turnips, and greens. Ah! what a rush there used to be for the greens. You might sometimes get hot rolls; but, generally speaking, I bought the Turkish bread (*ekmek*), baked at Balaclava.

Mary Seacole is the first of the extracts on the subject of home and in many ways offers a rich starting point for the study of shifts and changes in the depiction of home through autobiographical writings. For her home would have been a concept with complicated connotations. She can be viewed in the light of the Black African diaspora caused by European empire-building, therefore, home was something stolen and then replaced on the other side of the Atlantic. Home appears here, in her description of the Crimea during conflict, as an aspiration, something to capture or create for the serving soldiers.

The context of war is vital here; allow your students to explore how the details Seacole offers relate to the immediate context of war. This can then be placed in the context of the way that she shows an awareness of her audience. There isn't the factual tone of journalistic writing that we hear today from the frontline – details of casualties and losses. Nor is there any sense of implied criticism of the war. Seacole writes in a way that seems to be designed to offer reassurances that conditions are not so bad. Comparisons with contemporary journalism or with the *Wipers Times* published on the frontline during World War I will be revealing steps to take.

By looking at semantic field your students will start to build a picture of the notion of 'home away from home' that Seacole describes. The list of provisions is the key here. Home is established through goods for the 'outer man' and the 'inner man'. It is through this sustenance of the body that home is created. Maybe one can detect a sense of maternal behaviour in this description of home too – home is not a place but a relationship based on love and care.

Maybe there is a sense of personal vindication in this extract too. In later extracts we can trace the ways that writers are using autobiographical writings to describe or create a place in the world. Here, some readers may feel that as a response to her rejection by authority and society Mary Seacole is writing herself in to the story of the Crimea through her accounts of the incredible work she did there.

Robert Falcon Scott, *The Journals of Captain RF Scott* (1913)

The English naval officer and explorer Robert Falcon Scott arrived at the South Pole on 18 January 1912 to find that a Norwegian expedition lead by Roald Amundsen had already beaten him there.

The following extracts from his journals are amongst the last entries before his death on the treacherous journey back home. His temporary home is his tent.

Wednesday, March 21 – Got within 11 miles of depot Monday night; had to lay up all yesterday in severe blizzard. To-day forlorn hope, Wilson and Bowers going to depot for fuel.

Thursday, March 22 and 23 – Blizzard bad as ever – Wilson and Bowers unable to start – to-morrow last chance – no fuel and only one or two of food left – must be near the end. Have decided it shall be natural – we shall march for the depot with or without our effects and die in our tracks.

Thursday, March 29 – Since the 21st we have had a continuous gale from WSW and SW We had fuel to make two cups of tea apiece and bare food for two days on the 20th. Every day we have been ready to start for our depot 11 miles away, but outside the door of the tent it remains a scene of whirling drift. I do not think that we can hope for better things now. We shall stick it out to the end, but we are getting weaker, of course, and the end cannot be far.

It seems a pity, but I do not think that I can write more.

R. SCOTT

One of the themes that we hope to develop in this sequence of extracts is the idea of home being incarcerating or claustrophobic. Here is a 'home' from which Scott and his men are desperate to escape.

An opening discussion about audience and purpose would prove profitable here. Why is Scott writing all this down? What does he want his audience to think or feel when reading this journal?

Semantics is an area that can be usefully explored here. Scott demonstrates the British reserve in expressions like 'I do not think that we can hope for better things now' and 'It seems a pity ... ' What is implicitly being suggested here? Death is a difficult subject to write bluntly about. 'Better things' here means living, 'the end' means death.

Grammar is another area that can be explored. Discussing the role of grammatical structures and their impact upon meanings is often a subject that students find difficult to write about. This text offers some fairly clear insights into grammar. Scott writes in a kind of grammatical shorthand. His sentences are truncated contractions. In his entry for Thursday, 22 and 23 March, he employs hyphens to demark sentences. This gives the sense of the writing being hurried or less important than the following entry dated Thursday, 29th. Here the standard sentence structures return and this imposes a sense of the writing being crafted. The pace of the piece slows and the language choices appear more measured. The writing appears to have had more of the attention of the writer. Perhaps this indicates that Scott has truly given up at this point and has resigned himself to his inevitable demise. Are the grammatical errors, *bare food* and *no fuel and only one or two of food left*, signs of exhaustion?

There are always lexical items in a text that can be looked at in isolation. How about *effects* here? Or *pity*? Sometimes it is the seemingly insignificant words that are worthy of attention and to examine such words closely is good training for the investigative linguist. The word *it* is used here to mean opposing things. In the sentence *Have decided it shall be natural* he is talking about death whilst in the expression *We shall stick it out* he means life.

Robert Graves, *Goodbye to All That* (1929)

Robert Graves, having survived World War I, came home to a disrupted country and life that would forever be affected by the legacy of conflict. He continued with the academic pursuits that he was engaging with prior to seeing action as a serving officer as well as continuing with the rest of his life.

> My mother, in letting us the Islip house, put a clause in the agreement that it must be used as a residence only, and not for the carrying on of any trade or business. She wanted to guard herself against any further commercial enterprise on our part; but need not have worried – we have learned our lesson. Islip, an agricultural village, lay far enough from Oxford not to be contaminated with the roguery for which the outskirts of most university towns are notorious. The policeman led an easy life. During the four years we lived there nothing of ours was ever stolen, and no Islip cottager cheated or offended us. Once, by mistake, I left my bicycle at the station for two days and, when I recovered it, not only were both lamps, the pump, and the repair outfit still in place, but an anonymous friend had even cleaned it.

In this passage Graves speaks of his move to a new home using the language of legal transactions. There is the formality seen in Mary Seacole's writing, though here it is less intimate. Graves' tone, exemplified by 'clause in the agreement' and 'commercial enterprise', is used to describe the agreement made over the property as well as being an indicator of the social relationships at the time. To locate a sense of time and place through close linguistic analysis is a skill that your students will naturally possess; by providing them with stimulating texts you can nudge them further along their journey to becoming independent thinkers.

Taking the individual's personal contexts, the wider social contexts and the ever-present historical context of the legacy of war, one can see compelling readings of Graves' semantic fields. Once past the first two sentences the extract changes. The semantic field of pastoral life permeates the piece, 'agricultural village', 'easy life', 'cottager' and 'bicycle' all contribute to the creation of a rural idyll. He is describing the world he now inhabits and simultaneously he captures a moment in the development of society and language for us to study. Your students can explore other writers from the period to analyse whether there were widespread attempts to distance society from the disruptions of war. They can compare connotations of 'cottager' in a 1929 autobiography with the layers of meanings that lexical item has today. Equally, Graves' use of 'agricultural' differs from a football commentator using the term today, to mean crude or even dangerous play.

As a piece of discourse that captures a historical moment Graves offers us a glimpse into a world that no longer exists. It looks pretty much the same, the words certainly look and sound the same, but it has gone. Even the description of the bike's accessories, the 'lamps' and 'repair outfit' are archaisms in that context though the lexical items themselves still function in various forms today. As the extract has been chosen to exemplify notions of home in autobiographical writing, we should finish with a few words on that subject.

The 'residence' described doesn't seem like home, just a building. Home isn't described through senses or relationships. What the writer offers us is a nostalgic and distant vision of the notion of home as an idea in which community and society are the foundations of a home. Graves' anecdote is a discourse feature that signifies a wider discourse about seeking a way of life that is different from the grim legacy of World War I. A world that is not only crime-free but where mysterious strangers repair misplaced objects. The point is *Goodbye to All That* is a rich text in itself for its semantic fields and as a glimpse of language and worlds that are gone.

Herman Hesse, *On Moving to a New House* (1931)

This extract, which appears here in translation from the original German, takes a different narrative stance to Graves' text. Hesse offers a view of moving house which is much more intimate, more personally revealing than Graves. Perhaps here we can see a style closer to Ellen MacArthur or William Feinnes; it is a modern text focused closely on the writer's mind and the psychological construction of the world.

> Moving to a new house means not only beginning something new but giving up something old as well. And now as I move to our new house I can, of course, feel gratitude from the bottom of my heart to the kind people that gave us this house, I think with thankfulness and renewed friendship of him and of the other friends who joined together to help with the building and furnishing. But to make a statement about the new house, to present it in a narrative, to praise it, to sing a song to it, that I would not be able to do, for how is one to compose words and sing songs at the first step of a new undertaking, how is one to celebrate a day before evening comes? At the dedication of a new house we can, of course, cherish hopes in our hearts and urge our friends to carry in their own hearts unspoken wishes for the future of the house and of our lives. However, to say anything about the new house, to give real news about it, to declare any relationship to it, that is something that I could do only after a year and a day.

Starting with the narrative, the discourse features of the piece, you can guide students to compare the outlook on the world offered here to the previous texts. It is about creating and experiencing joy and harmony in life, it looks to the future, 'beginning something new' and choosing to make up his mind about the house 'after a year and a day.' The optimism can then be traced through Hesse's semantic field.

His register is one of emotional openness and exploration. The list of lexical choices that can be completed in class begins with, 'gratitude', 'bottom of my heart', 'kind', 'thankfulness', 'friendship' and 'joined together'. Regarding this list through the contextual lens of social and political history the interest in the text becomes clearer. Economic depression caused by the legacy of World War I had made Germany a tough place to live for many people. Maybe Hesse's passage is closer to Graves' than it first appears. But rather than retrospective sentimentalism he opts for a visionary description of how things could be. In both texts the semantic fields reveal interesting relationships between historical contexts and writers' perspectives.

Grammatically the use of a rhetorical question sits with the modern idea of the individual being paramount. He invites personal reflections in response to his question through both the interrogative form itself and the use of the pronoun 'one'. Compared to Graves' attempts to create a sense of community, it seems Hesse is constructing a more individualistic world.

There are many further activities that can be undertaken using this extract as a starting point. Collecting a range of other texts published in 1931, newspaper articles from web archives, literary texts, advertisements and speeches could all be used to challenge the readings of this text offered up by close linguistic analysis. Let your students take their own routes through the historical developments of language and see where they take each other.

Nelson Mandela, *Long Walk to Freedom* (1994)

In 1990 Nelson Mandela was released from 27 years of confinement in prison. He published *Long Walk to Freedom* in 1994 and detailed his life from childhood to his inauguration as President of South Africa. The following passage recounts the phase of his release where, though still imprisoned, he has his own 'home'.

> The next day I surveyed my new abode and discovered a swimming pool in the backyard, and two smaller bedrooms. I walked outside and admired the trees that shaded the house and kept it cool. The entire place felt removed, isolated. The only thing spoiling the idyllic picture was that the walls were topped with razor wire, and there were guards at the entrance to the house. Even so, it was a lovely place and situation; a halfway house between prison and freedom.
>
> That afternoon I was visited by Kobie Coetsee, who brought a case of Cape wine as a housewarming gift. The irony of a jailer bringing his prisoner such a gift was not lost on either of us. He was extremely solicitous and wanted to make sure that I liked my new home. He surveyed the house himself, and the only thing he recommended was that the walls outside the house be raised – for my privacy, he said. He told me that the cottage at Victor Verster would be my last home before becoming a free man. The reason behind this move, he said, was that I should have a place where I could hold discussions in privacy and comfort.
>
> The cottage did in fact give me the illusion of freedom. I could go to sleep and wake up as I pleased, swim whenever I wanted, eat when I was hungry – all were delicious sensations. Simply to be able to go outside during the day and take a walk when I desired was a moment of private glory. There were no bars on the windows, no jangling keys, no doors to lock or unlock. It was altogether pleasant, but I never forgot that it was a gilded cage.

Mandela's description disrupts notions of home. His 'abode' has some features of a rather luxurious home but the swimming pool and cool shade, whilst offering respite from the baking South African sun, are far from homely. Home is not a place then, and the subtleties in this extract offer rich opportunities for discussion of how we are able to communicate and understand abstract concepts.

Presented with this passage your students have an opportunity to explore lexical choices. The range of choices for the place in which he resides includes 'abode', 'place', 'house', 'halfway house', 'home', 'cottage' and 'gilded cage'. With knowledge of the context these choices demonstrate a sense of uncertainty and instability. This is precisely what makes the study of language change through theme (e.g. home) interesting; your students will understand that it is only when a text is examined in the contexts of production and reception that the shifting nature of language can be seen. Mandela's autobiography is showing your students a precise example of how a writer, using a shared language, can change the ways that words are meant.

Grammatically, Mandela's use of sub-clauses also demonstrates something precise about the contextual factors governing the range of meanings in this short passage. Twice he repeats the phrase 'he said'. Here is a point of grammatical interest that can be explained as a demonstration of the ways that language changes. Mandela has the right to challenge the political authorities that have 'caged' him for so long and he expresses his refusal to accept what they tell him through his grammatical constructions. Noun phrases such as 'delicious sensations', verb choices like 'surveyed', and repetition in the penultimate sentence are further grammatical features to explore as demonstrations of how language change is present in all of the frameworks of English.

William Feinnes, *The Snow Geese* (2001)

William Fiennes' *The Snow Geese* was published in 2001. The book focuses on Fiennes' convalescence after treatment for cancer. He returns to live with his parents. His bedroom has a dormer window through which, whilst lying in bed, he observes the movements of both homing and migratory birds, becoming fascinated by snow geese. Fiennes considers the opposing pulls of going home and the need to leave.

Here is the extract for analysis.

I waited for my condition to improve. I wasn't patient. The edge of my fear rubbed off as the weeks passed, but I became depressed. In hospital I had longed to return to the environment I knew better than any other, because it was something of which I could be sure; because the familiar — the *known* — promised sanctuary from all that was confusing, alien, and new. But after a while the complexion of the familiar began to change. The house, and the past it contained, seemed more prison than sanctuary. As I saw it, my friends were proceeding with their lives, their appetites and energies undimmed, while I was being held back against my will, penalized for an offence of which I was entirely ignorant. My initial relief that the crisis had passed turned slowly to anger, and my frustrations were mollified but not resolved by the kindness of those close to me, because no one, however loving, could give me the one thing I wanted above all else: my former self.

Leaves hid the nests in the tree crowns. Swallows returned in April, followed by swifts in May. After supper we'd sit out at the back of the house, watching swifts wheel overhead on their vespers flights, screaming parties racing in the half-light. Rooks flew in feeding sorties from the wood to the fields. You could hear the Sor Brook coursing over the waterfall in the trees, the sibilance of congregations saying *trespasses, trespasses, forgive us our trespasses*. But the sound was no longer a source of comfort. I couldn't relax into the necessity for this confinement. I felt the loss not just of my strength but of my capacity for joy. I tried to concentrate on the swifts, to pin my attention to something other than my own anxieties. I knew that generation after generation returned to the same favoured nesting sites, and that these were most likely the same birds we had watched the year before, descendants of swifts that had nested in the eaves of the house when my mother and father first moved to it; descendants, too, of swifts my father had watched as a boy, visiting his grandparents in the same house.

One activity that you could try here is that of creating semantic fields. Ask each student (or group of students) to create a list of words that they think they can gather together. It might be a thematic link or perhaps a particular word class that they think is important to the text. It might be a set of technical terms from some area of life. Students should report back to the whole group. With a collection of such reports, students should be able to get closer to the essence of the piece.

Ellen MacArthur, *blog.ellenmacarthur.com* (2009)

To finish our sequence of extracts of autobiography we have a blog from Ellen MacArthur, the sailor and adventurer. Here is the text for analysis.

Busy Few Weeks

Well, the past few weeks have been pretty busy really. We went to see a sustainable housing development in South London called BedZed, and spent the weekend trying out a few new ideas on the energy front. BedZed was really interesting; amazingly it was designed 10 years ago as a zero energy development – with solar gain for space heating (using the windows), there are office blocks with windows to the north and houses with windows to the south, there is no other space heating whatsoever, and there are roof gardens and rain water harvesting. There are other developments I am very keen to have a look at – there is so much learning to do!!

At home in Cowes I have fitted a sun pipe in my flat. It's designed to let light into the flat through any loft space, creating a skylight effect where you can't fit a skylight. It's a small flat glass window on the outside, and a silver foil tunnel bringing light through the roof space or loft to the ceiling of the lower room. In a relatively dark and dingy flat, the feeling has completely changed. The sun pipe brings in floods of light – and for the first time in the day I was able to work at my computer without the lights on! Fitting it was pretty easy – I've filmed it – so I'll get the video online soon. Just a few tiles off the roof, a bit of insulation moved out of the way, a hole in the plasterboard ceiling, then the bottom clipped in! Awesome

I've also been doing some tests to see what power consumption of a kettle, or a fridge is like... ... It certainly depends on the type of kettle you have, but mine costs 0.5p for a pint, which is about right for 2 nice big mugs of tea... Funnily enough I thought that it would cost more than this. I guess if you live alone and have 4 cups of tea a day that's roughly 1p a day, which works out at £3.65 per year on day time tariff. However if you multiply the kettle by 55 people at work, and 4 cups a day – then you get into the £200 per year area ... which if using too much water – that could easily escalate to £400 or £500

Ellen

26 comments have been made

This extract offers the opportunity to discuss the way in which the technology of blogs and the internet more widely, has changed the genre of autobiographical writing. It is part of that new hybrid form of communication that is somewhere between speech and writing.

An immediately striking feature of this text is the new relationship between writer and reader that is created by the technology. The opportunity for the reader to comment upon what is there is anticipated by the writer. Indeed, Ellen MacArthur actively poses questions to elicit responses to help her with her home improvements.

Another feature of the text that I find distinctive here is the conversational voice. The casual tone of the lexis and the use of ellipsis and dashes as grammar breaks indicate a personal relationship that is imagined rather than real. The immediacy of the text and the supposed logging of daily events create an intimacy for the reader.

One feature that this text shares with earlier autobiographies is the writer's assumption that their life is worthy of recording in this way. This is highlighted here because of the day-to-day nature of the subject content. In contrast to Scott's last words in exploring Polar Regions, here we read about Ellen MacArthur's attempts to be eco-friendly in her house.

Perhaps all of the above features can be linked to the way we perceive the internet as a communication form. Personal communications via email, Facebook and the like tend to be throwaway by nature. Perhaps MacArthur's tone and content in this extract exemplify this attitude.

Chapter 8

Language acquisition

Pre-teaching thinking

Choosing a beginning point for teaching Children's Language Acquisition is a complex decision. There are many different points that can be chosen and all have distinct benefits. You need to consider some questions to decide how you feel about structuring the course in order to meet the needs of your students and the demands of your chosen exam board's specifications.

1   Do I teach the acquisition of language in a linear way, tracing development from before birth to the end of the critical period?
2   Do I teach the stages of development in each framework as discrete strands?
3   To what extent do I merge the strands of development of reading and writing and spoken language?
4   Do I teach theoretical perspectives first or wait until later in the course?
5   Do I have a tendency to accept the work of certain theorists over others? Do I teach one as more 'correct' than another or present a balanced overview?

Your responses to these questions contain your ideological assumptions about how children acquire language. Extending your thoughts to a discussion with your colleagues will create an opportunity to develop a cohesive departmental approach to this unit.

This section of the book is designed to give you a range of ideas for teaching that can be adopted in different ways and delivered in different orders until your preferred method of teaching the course is realised.

The hermeneutic circle

Children's language acquisition is an area of linguistic study like any other; constituent parts can only be understood in the context of the full picture and the full picture can only be understood through the understanding of its constituent parts. The choices that you will make based on the questions posed above will begin to address the difficult question 'Where should I start?'

The processes involved in speaking first words are deeply complex and to understand them one must take into account a range of influencing factors. Let's take the utterance 'mummy' as an example. Imagine the scene: Molly is 17 months old. She is in the living room with her mother and father, there are toys and books everywhere and both parents are playing with their daughter.

FATHER: Where's Molly's cat? (2) Where's your cat, Molly?
MOLLY: Mummy
FATHER: Has mummy got your cat?

In this single word utterance Molly is demonstrating a number of explainable language acquisition skills and exploring them exemplifies why starting points are flexible.

1   It is likely that Molly is repeating a lexical item that she has repeatedly heard in the first 17 months of her life. She may also have encountered 'mummy' in stories.
2   Molly shows that, though beyond her ability to speak, she has an understanding of the questions that she has been asked.
3   Molly demonstrates her ability to take her turn in a conversation.
4   We can assume that, with a glance, pointing or other paralinguistic feature, she is communicating rather than automatically repeating a lexical item. Her father's response implies the understanding that he has of her utterance.
5   A child's physiological development affects their phonological capability. It is noteworthy that in this bi-syllabic utterance one phoneme is repeated and this repeated sound is the beginning of each syllable. Furthermore, the repeated sound is made by blocking the passage of air with the lips which form the furthest forward part of the mouth.
6   Grammatically, Molly shows some awareness of the interrogative form that her father's utterance employs.
7   The context of this interaction affects our ability to understand, especially, Molly's contribution.

Though not exhaustive, this list suggests that this area of linguistic study is rich and diverse.

Suggested route

So there is no clear starting point from which all subsequent study is developed; this leaves you with the prospect of introducing students to areas of this unit that they will not fully understand until they are some way through their studies. The clearest advice that I can give here is that you embrace this reality and that you openly and clearly explain this situation to your students. All knowledge gained in lessons and through private study and research forms a part of an accumulative body of knowledge. With each step that is taken embedded knowledge is made more detailed and should be used to review old notes and annotated transcripts. This approach ensures that the entire body of knowledge is available, to be drawn upon at all points during the course and that the interplay between points on a language acquisition 'timeline' and the linguistic frameworks being adopted is constantly under review. This methodology means that your students will be prepared to actively think when faced with an examination text rather than being 'taught' how to write examination responses.

The sounds of language acquisition

Your students do not need to learn all of the phonemic symbols that relate to the sounds that make up the English language. They do, however, need to be familiar with the way that they are transcribed and be able to read the symbols in transcribed interactions between speakers.

Table 2: Phonemic symbols

Consonants		Short vowels	
p	p<u>ip</u>	ɪ	p<u>i</u>t
b	<u>bib</u>	ɛ	p<u>e</u>t
t	<u>t</u>en	æ	p<u>a</u>t
d	<u>d</u>en	ɒ	p<u>o</u>t
k	<u>c</u>at	ʌ	p<u>u</u>tt
g	<u>g</u>et	ʊ	p<u>u</u>t
f	<u>f</u>ish	ə	patt<u>er</u>
v	<u>v</u>an		
θ	<u>th</u>igh	*Long vowels*	
ð	<u>th</u>y		
s	<u>s</u>et	i:	b<u>ea</u>n
z	<u>z</u>en	ɜ:	b<u>ur</u>n
ʃ	<u>sh</u>ip	ɑ:	b<u>ar</u>n
ʒ	lei<u>s</u>ure	ɔ:	b<u>or</u>n
h	<u>h</u>en	u:	b<u>oo</u>n
tʃ	<u>ch</u>ur<u>ch</u>		
dʒ	<u>j</u>u<u>dg</u>e	*Dipthongs*	
m	<u>m</u>an		
n	ma<u>n</u>	aɪ	b<u>i</u>te
ŋ	si<u>ng</u>	ɛɪ	b<u>ai</u>t
l	<u>l</u>et	ɔɪ	b<u>oy</u>
r	<u>r</u>ide	əʊ	r<u>oe</u>
w	<u>w</u>et	aʊ	h<u>ou</u>se
j	<u>y</u>et	ʊə	p<u>oor</u>
		ɪə	<u>ear</u>
		ɛə	<u>air</u>

The most effective apparatus that we have available to us in the classroom to gain the required level of expertise over this data is our voices. Playing with these sounds allows students to feel where sounds come from and to hear the sounds as they appear when isolated from the sounds that surround them in everyday speech.

Our names are some of the most familiar sounds that we hear spoken and provide us with an ideal beginning for studying the phonology of acquiring language.

Idea one

Use your name as a model of how to translate a lexical item into a chain of phonemic symbols:

NICHOLAS = nɪkʊlʊs

It is immediately clear that eight letters are reduced to seven distinct sounds. The sounds need to be spoken clearly so that the students can hear the distinct elements that constitute your name. This activity can then be repeated by students, in pairs, and the products of their interactions can be shared with the whole class. By using names as an example it creates the opportunity for the most familiar of words to be defamiliarised. In itself, this is interesting as it allows students to see and hear language in a new way. There is also the deeper effect of creating a sense of empathy with a very young child acquiring speech: everything is new and has to be learned.

Idea two

This activity can be developed as a small group task. Students can:

1   Write each other short messages.
2   'Translate' a given text from standard alphabet to phonemic symbols.
3   'Translate' a given text from phonemic symbols to standard alphabet.
4   Respond to a set of given questions using phonemic symbols.

The possibilities are inexhaustible.

Idea three

To bridge this introduction to phonemic symbols and children's language acquisition ask the questions 'What were your first words?' and 'What do you think are the commonest first words a child speaks?' Common and often correct responses may include 'mummy', 'daddy', 'teddy', 'bear' or 'bye bye'.

Your investigation into why certain words appear in a child's lexicon as first words has just begun. Ask the students in small groups to develop the initial list of three or four words and to consider ways in which they might be able to group the words. Offering a hint that remembering the linguistic frameworks they have become familiar with is a good starting point. They may offer some or all of the following suggestions, they may well offer more imaginative responses than we are able to predict.

Possible responses

1   They are words that are often heard.
2   They are nouns and so can be visualised in the world around them.
3   The words relate to their favourite or loved things and people.
4   They are easy to say.
5   They are useful to the child.

This leads to an opportunity for students to learn about the place and manner of articulation of English consonant sounds, which leads to the next stage of learning about the acquisition of reading and writing skills.

Introduce your students to the diagram detailing the **places of articulation**. These are the different areas of the mouth and throat that we use to make different sounds. If you have access to the internet in your lessons there is an excellent resource on www.chass.utoronto. ca/~danhall/phonetics/sammy.html that can be manipulated and adapted to show what we do with our vocal tracts to create different sounds.

Students can learn a great deal without it though, because making noises, repeating them, feeling inside your own mouth with your tongue or finger, isolating sounds and saying them quickly and slowly, effectively consciously repeating the learning processes, are the very best ways of learning about a child's phonological development.

Give students the simple piece of knowledge that children's first sounds are made using parts of the body at the front of the vocal tract and sounds formed from the back of the vocal tract are mastered later. Allowing students to play around with making sounds for a while and asking them to record some initial thoughts will mean that they can discover for themselves how sounds are made.

Finally, return to the question that was asked at the beginning and observe how the students' responses have developed.

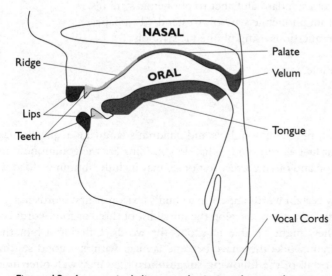

Figure 13: Anatomical diagram depicting the vocal system

This diagram, adapted from www.gamasutra.com/view/feature/3179/read_my_lips_ facial_animation_.php?page=2 is appropriately detailed and allows for a perfectly satisfactory understanding of the different parts of the mouth used to create sounds. Students will never be tested by being asked to label a blank version. There are many reasons to be familiar with the most-used terminology, from the parts of the vocal system, front to back.

The use of these terms is valuable for the following purposes:

1   To understand the places of articulation.
2   To appreciate one reason for the order of acquisition of lexical items.
3   To explain common difficulties in articulating certain phonemes.
4   To facilitate understanding of learning to read.
5   To combine with knowledge that will be subsequently gained about other areas of acquisition.
6   To develop their technical vocabularies.

To bring this knowledge to life, and to ensure that different areas of understanding are connecting together, this diagram can be used alongside an activity. Using the phonemic symbols, try to map out which sounds are made using just the lips, and then travel back through the vocal system noting how different parts of the system are used. In the earliest stages of creating sounds, children develop sounds from the front of the system first, for instance words such as 'mummy' and 'daddy'. Realising that these words which occur so early in a child's lexicon for social reasons are also traceable through an understanding of phonological development is an important leap in your students' grasp of phonology.

Idea four: Working with transcripts

A clear understanding of the acquisition of spoken language is made simple through the use of transcripts of real conversations between parents and children. These transcripts demonstrate how young children develop their abilities with language and then how they make their new-found skills work to their advantage. The transcripts allow us to see the way that children gain attention, make requests and make sense of the language.

The transcripts used for assessment by examination boards are always selected for their usefulness in having 'features' that can be spotted. The student needs to be alert to ways in which they can bring their theoretical learning into practice. For example:

> MOTHER:(reading from a book) It's a ...
> CARLY: Bootar
> MOTHER:No (.) it's a scooter (.) say scoo (.) ter
> CARLY: Bootar
> MOTHER:No (.) silly Carly (.) it's a scooter.
> **Key:** (.) indicates brief pause

Here, the mother is instinctively trying to teach her child. She wants Carly to pronounce the word scooter accurately. Carly can't quite get her mouth to do this yet. Theory suggests (Nelson) that Carly will iron this out in time and that no amount of correcting by mother is going to make any difference. Indeed, Nelson would suggest that correcting a child will actively get in the way of language development. This is the sort of 'feature' that is there to be 'spotted'. Here is a further example:

> CARLY: We wented to park (.) sheeps dada
> *Key:* (.) indicates brief pause

In this utterance there are two examples of the child's ability to learn language, specifically to grasp and make use of grammatical patterns. Chomsky feels that, whilst children copy the language around them, they have an innate ability to process lexical items into grammatical patterns. Parents do not teach their children grammar. Here, through two 'mistakes', we can see that Carly has learnt the patterns of 'ed' for the past tense and 's' for a plural. The irregular nature of the word 'go' in the past tense and 'sheep' as a plural have caught Carly out but they demonstrate her developing ability. Again, this is the sort of 'feature' that will be in exam pieces to be spotted and remarked upon.

Here is an example of a stretch of genuine conversation that offers the potential for discussion of how language is being made to function by and with children.

> *Key:* (.) indicates brief pause

Numbers within brackets indicates length of pause in seconds. Other contextual information is in italics in square brackets.

David (father) is getting Mickey ready for bed while Rose (mother) is present in the same room feeding Mickey's younger brother Jack. David is reading Mickey a well-known bedtime story.

	DAVID:	'That's a giraffe isn't it? (2) Is that a giraffe?'
	MICKEY:	'Hiya (3) Mama'
	DAVID:	'What's that?'
	MICKEY:	'Mama'
5	DAVID:	'Do you want to read a book? (1) what do you want to read?'
	MICKEY:	'Shoowawa'
	DAVID:	'Shall we read this one?'
	MICKEY:	'Mmmm'
	DAVID:	'Is that a train?'
10	ROSE:	'Is that choo-choo?'
	MICKEY:	'Yeah (4) yeah (1) yeah'
	DAVID:	'That's the train isn't it?'
	MICKEY:	'Choo-choo'
	ROSE:	'Goodboy'
15	DAVID:	'And that's a tractor'
	MICKEY:	'Yeah'
	DAVID:	'Goodboy'
	MICKEY:	'Dooda'
	DAVID:	'Yeah'
20	MICKEY:	'Dooda'
	DAVID:	'Yeah is that another one?'
	MICKEY:	'Dooda'

	DAVID:	'Shall we show the train to your brother?'
	MICKEY:	'Baba'
25	DAVID:	'Show Jack'
	MICKEY:	'Dooda'
	ROSE:	'Goodboy'
	DAVID:	'Where's the banana?'
	MICKEY:	'Da! (2) da!'
30	DAVID:	'Yeah that's cabbage'
	MICKEY:	'Coga (2) Mmmm mama (.) mama!'
	DAVID:	'What do you want now?'
	MICKEY:	'Dada (2) mama'
	DAVID:	'Where's the ball?'
35	MICKEY:	'Ba (2) nana?'
	DAVID:	'Look Jack's drinking his milk isn't he? (1) Is Baba drinking milk?'
	MICKEY:	'Baba!'
	DAVID:	'Who's that?
	MICKEY:	'Baba'

Key: (.) indicates brief pause

In this sequence there are a number of possible points of discussion.

One way of assessing what is happening here is to observe the individual speaker's contributions in isolation. The father, David, asks 16 questions in this short sequence. He is clearly, at first, trying to gain and keep the attention of Mickey. He also uses questions to get Mickey to respond to the book. In this way, Mickey is learning the need to contribute to the conversation. After all, the basic unit of a conversation is a turn. Questions require answers; Mickey is developing this part of his language production.

Mickey is also able to make requests and indicate his preferences in this sequence. He chooses to read a book and also requests the attention of his mother and asks if he can have a banana. Whilst his lexical choices are limited, Mickey is able to make himself clear.

Mickey has a preference for the sounds made by tractors and trains. 'Shoowawa', dooda' and 'choo choo' are more appealing than the utterances 'tractor' and 'train'. One function of language that is distinctly human is that we like to make sounds. Some sounds are more fun than others.

Positive reinforcement is thought to be important to language development. On line 27, Rose (mother) praises Mickey for showing the train to his brother.

Let's look at another transcript.

Kim (mother) is in the kitchen with Renee, Cole and Nina. They are having lunch.

	NINA:	'Mummy dummy gone dummy gone (.) Mummy find it (.) I find it here.
	KIM:	'Cole you want yog-yog?'
	NINA:	'Cole me find it (.) yeah'
	COLE:	'My want yog-yog'
5	RENEE:	'Right (.) Neen you're allowed one yog-yog after you have finished your yummy dinner!'
	NINA:	'Mmmm (4) Mummy!' [*Nina does not eat any more of her dinner*]

	RENEE:	'Good girl Neens (.) good girl (3) Mummy am I allowed a yoghurt please? I finished all mine!'
10	KIM:	'Yep'
	RENEE:	'Mummy do I have to have to have a yoghurt because I don't want one (.) am I allowed crisps please?'
	KIM:	'You can have a packet of crisps if you like because you've been a good girl hasn't she Nina?' (3) Has Renee been a good girl and eaten all her dinner? (.)
15		Yes she has (.)
	RENEE:	'Neens you have crisps if you finish yummy dinner (.) yeah?'
	NINA:	'yeah (.) muumy!'
	RENEE:	'Mummy Sarah says she wants me to come to her house for a sleepover (.) am I allowed to go?'
20	KIM:	'We'll see darling, but grandma's round tonight!'
	RENEE:	'Ow mummy (.) but everyone's having sleepovers'
	KIM:	'We'll see.'
	RENEE:	'You promise?'
	KIM:	'Yes I promise (.) I'll think about it'
	RENEE:	'When?'
	KIM:	'Soon (.) Are you ready for your crisps now madam?'
	RENEE:	'When mummy? (.) yeah'

Key: (.) indicates brief pause

Idea five

To measure understanding so far, and to address the greater demand for creative thought and writing in the new A level specifications, getting your students to write a book for young children is a very productive process.

Set up the task with basic audience/purpose parameters. The age and gender of the children for whom the book is written, the nature of the text – whether it is to be read to children or to help them to learn to read – and the content of the book are all to be decided by students. When the writing and book production are finished all of these choices will have to be justified and explained in relation to the book that they have written.

Conscious awareness of why everything that is included in the book is there is vital to the success of this project. Planning, therefore, is key to deep learning taking place. How the students undertake their planning is your choice; you can decide to explain the task verbally and let the students go or the planning stages can be formalised.

Planning grid: writing for young children

AUDIENCE – AGE, GENDER …

PURPOSE(S) – BEDTIME, TEACHING TOOL, INTERACTION, EDUCATION …

CHARACTERS

PLOT/NARRATIVE/DEVELOPMENT THROUGH TEXT

STORYBOARD

1	2	3	4
5	6	7	8
9	10	11	12
13	14	15	16

Teaching children to read and write

Pre-teaching thinking

The second component to the language acquisition module deals with the teaching of reading and writing to young children. Whilst the acquisition of speaking skills is seen to be partly innate, reading and writing are artificial skills that need actively to be taught. This fact can often lead students to assume that the child's acquisition of reading and writing is more difficult for them than the acquisition of speech. Students need to be encouraged to consider the development of these very different skills separately. In truth, the development of reading and writing is a much smaller and less sophisticated achievement than the mastery of speech; merely the written production of sounds and the recognition of sound symbols (letters and words).

Your students need the opportunity to think through a number of issues here:

1   How a child might be introduced to the ideas of reading and writing.
2   What sort of approaches are currently in use to teach these skills.
3   Why there is such debate about how to teach writing, and in particular, reading.
4   How to find and consider theoretical studies.

Reading

We have considered elsewhere in this book the idea that meaning does not reside within words themselves but in their applications. This idea can be related to whole texts as well. Our approach to poetry as a form of literature exemplifies this. Readers are often encouraged to examine what a poem means to them rather than what they think the poet meant by the poem. GCSE specifications tend to reward this sort of reflection. However, poetry aside, we seem to pursue meanings that are inherently within texts when considering other forms of writing: novels, plays, books of history etc. This kind of search for meaning elevates the importance of the writer and the text whilst relegating the importance of the reader. The reader, however, brings whole sets of cultural and personal experiences to the text. This has never been more so than now in our post-modern world. Information is at the fingertips of all of us. How we interpret that information is of primary importance. If we begin to follow this type of thinking then the role of the reader needs to be re-interpreted.

The reader does not search for and confirm meanings in the text but creates meanings with the text as a starting point rather than an end point. This makes perfect sense. Joining a reading club would be a very dull hobby if we didn't interpret books in varying ways. This sort of postmodernist thinking surely has very real applications for the teaching of reading.

Initially, of course, children need to be taught to recognise the meaning of the written symbols that represent letters and sounds. There is a great deal of debate about how this is to be achieved.

As you can see from the extract of the article opposite, there is no real agreement about how or even when reading should be taught. I think that the healthiest way for your students to consider this area is for them to research the various approaches that are currently being used. This might involve visiting your local primary schools to find out which approaches are actually taking place.

So how should teachers teach reading?

Jim Rose, in his interim review of the National Literacy Strategy (2005) has been careful to avoid what he describes as a 'futile debate' over which strategies are most effective but he does recommend that synthetic phonics should be the first strategy teachers use, as it 'is the most effective, systematic approach to teaching reading.'

However, not everyone agrees that synthetic phonics is the answer to teaching children to read. Critics point out that English spelling is full of irregularities and that children must be given a comprehensive selection of strategies to decode text successfully. They also argue that advocates of synthetic phonics can't agree on exactly how to teach it, as Mike Baker points out in his BBC report 'Phonics: Strategy but no consensus' (December 2005).

This lack of consensus is further exacerbated by the findings of a new research study undertaken by Warwick University and led by Dr Jonathan Solity, which claims that children can master the basics of reading by learning just 100 words. (TES, 9 December 2005). The researchers argue that children who are taught these 100 words find it much easier to cope with real books and make sense of the new words they encounter, rather than by memorising the 150 words at KS1 and a further 100 at KS2, as currently recommended by the National Literacy Strategy.

Moreover, there really isn't much comfort to be had for those who rely on reading schemes as Dr Solity (2003), in a paper delivered to a DfES phonics seminar, also highlighted the work undertaken by the Early Reading Research, which seriously questions the effectiveness of teaching children to read by using reading schemes.

Where do we go from here?

So, despite Jim Rose's wish to avoid being dragged into a debate over how to teach children to read, it looks as if the battle will continue to rage for quite some time yet. However, he has agreed to investigate Dr Solity's research and take its findings into account by the time he makes his final report. Yet, while all this is going on, teachers still have to help children achieve the Early Learning goals of 'Exploring and experimenting with sounds, words and texts; reading a range of familiar and common words and simple sentences independently and knowing that print carries meaning and, in English, is read from left to right and top to bottom.'

Perhaps the best way to do this is to draw on what research has taught us about how the brain functions. To become good readers children need to be stimulated and excited by the reading process, as when a child's brain learns a new concept or skill, it creates a new neural network for it. This network can only be reinforced by repeated use and the best way to do this is to find fun ways of practising the new skill. This causes the brain to produce pleasure chemicals (endorphins), which naturally motivate the child to go on learning (Skelton, 1999). Therefore, when children are given the chance to learn to read in this way, they become focused and highly motivated learners.

> So, Professor Sylva's earlier assertion that reception teachers shouldn't teach children to read, isn't really relevant if we look at teaching reading as an enjoyable activity, which has the power to engage even very young children by using the way that their brains are naturally programmed to learn (Smilkstein 1993).
>
> (from www.teachingexpertise.com entitled 'the-great-how-and-when-to-teach-reading-debate)

There are a couple of important strands to the debate that can be simplified in the following ways:

- should children learn letters and sounds that are then used to blend into whole words (phonics) or should they be shown whole words and build up in this way their recognition of words (sight reading)?
- should the programme used be narrow and incremental without any other approaches or should a wide range of different approaches be used in tandem?

Theory and practice need to be considered side-by-side. Language acquisition presents an excellent chance for this type of research. In visiting schools and identifying how teachers approach the process of teaching reading may well help your students to view the theory in the right light. I think that students often accept theory as fact and do not always feel that they are allowed to have an opinion or that their findings are important. In an area like learning to read there is so much debate and disagreement that the theory and research that is published is often being challenged. Your students have here a real chance to form their own opinions about the theory, research and their own ideas.

Stages of development

Here is an area of research that students can easily locate. It might prove best for you to use one or two published and recognised theorists, such as Piaget, alongside more contemporary insights. The following list is taken from a website called 'kidslovelearning' and is a list given by a primary school teacher in the US to a parent. The list charts the development that she would expect a child to move through on the way to becoming a fluent reader.

Stages of reading

Emerging reader

ONE

Engages briefly with books shared one-on-one, relies on others to read or share books, begins to recognise some letters, recognises first name, recognises last name.

TWO

Enjoys having books read, enjoys looking at books on his/her own, repeats words from familiar books, makes up own story with books, identifies some letters, has an awareness of environmental print.

THREE

Responds to books read, begins to choose books on his/her own, retells story by looking at pictures after repeated listening experiences, knows how a book progresses from beginning to end, knows the difference between a letter and a word.

Early reader

FOUR

Engages in reading re-enactment, memorises some texts, shows directionality by running finger along lines of text (left-to-right and top-to-bottom), reproduces consonant sounds, uses initial consonants to identify words.

FIVE

Matches print words with spoken words, rereads familiar stories, reads self-created written messages, retells a familiar story without book, uses pictures as cues when reading text, predicts story events, words, and story endings, needs encouragement when reading new words or books, uses both initial and final consonants to identify words, knows what vowels are.

SIX

Reads using one-to-one correspondence and self-corrects errors, begins to develop fluency with familiar books, needs help to select appropriate reading material, builds on his/her high frequency sight word vocabulary, uses beginning, middle, and ending consonants to identify words.

Developing reader

SEVEN

Discusses and retells story to demonstrate understanding, compares or contrasts own experience with story, makes connections with other literature, reads new text one word at a time but shows some evidence of phrasing, corrects most errors that interfere with meaning, uses a variety of strategies when reading, comments on character, plot, and setting when prompted, chooses new, as well as, previously read books.

Begins to analyse words and make connections.

EIGHT

Reads fluently with expression most of the time, recognises errors , demonstrates comprehension of reading material through discussion and retelling, changes expression and inflection, answers and understands written questions, uses prior knowledge to make predictions, selects appropriate reading material, views self as reader, retells story.

NINE

Reads fluently with proper expression, rare mistakes, higher levels of thinking skills in comprehension, picks up nuances in books (humour, sadness, injustice, etc.), makes informed predictions using prior knowledge, makes connections independently, chooses to read for a variety of purposes, welcomes challenges as a reader.

The notion of stages may well prove popular with your students. It will sit well with the sequential stages of child language acquisition in terms of speech; babbling, single words, two-word gatherings, telegraphic talk, simple sentences.

One interesting debate that you and your students might enter into here is that of the role of the parent as opposed to the school. To what extent should the parent take responsibility for this nine-stage plan? If the parent values the act of reading and devotes time to reading with the child, how much will this increase the rate of development? If children are not taught the value of reading, which strands of the incremental plan will be harmed most?

A more general debate is to be had with the idea of the range of reading that a person needs to encounter in the modern world. Are traditional books still the best way to educate? What about online learning? Is the computer screen a more relevant way to educate children to read, both because they are likely to read a lot onscreen and there may well be a motivational edge to this form at the moment?

This represents a useful starting point in considering the core essentials of language recognition. You could have your students design books for children at different stages of the reading process. What are the needs of the emerging reader as opposed to the early or developing readers. Students could try to develop text that is based around using the 100-word hoard outlined above. You could even let them design books first then introduce the idea of the 100 words that research suggests will be most helpful in creating a critical mass of high frequency vocabulary.

Writing

Some introductory sequences

Ask the students to write their names on a blank piece of paper making use of their 'wrong' hand. Paper with no lines would be best to add to the struggle of producing something satisfactory. Having shared the results with each other, you could lead a discussion about why that is a difficult activity. It should become clear that the physical manipulation of the pen is not easy when you have not practised the motor skill required with that particular hand. Examine why you are able to write so much more confidently with the trained hand. How did you select the hand with which you write?

Hopefully, this activity and discussion will lead you and your students to the conclusion that the purpose of 'writing' in its earliest stages is to learn to manipulate the writing tool. A helpful analogy is that of riding a bicycle. You move from learning to cycle to employing that skill more usefully.

A second discussion that should prove fruitful is to consider how parents might introduce the idea of writing to their children. When are children first encouraged to manipulate writing implements? Do students feel that children should be able to produce letters and words before they go to school to be taught about such things? Are there any particular words that your students feel ought to be taught first? A broader question to consider would be how your students would set about teaching the skill of writing.

Your group may conclude that a child should begin school life with the ability to hold the writing tool 'properly' and perhaps be able to reproduce their own name. This would be a satisfactory conclusion to your early thinking about writing and a strong starting point for your consideration of formal attempts to teach writing.

Advice on engaging children in writing

There follows a parental advice sheet from CBeebies BBC television. Characterised here are stages from holding and manipulating writing implements through to copying letters and words. A clear emphasis is placed upon engaging the interest of children. The piece recognises that fun is part of the learning process if children are to succeed.

Learning to Write by Hannah Mortimer, Educational and Child Psychologist

- The first attempts at writing usually start at about the same time as the child starts playing with colours and painting (at about three years).
- At first their writing will be small scribbles and strokes on the paper consisting of circular lines and strokes.
- With help, children may be able to form the letters of their name using large print.
- Once your child knows how to trace letter shapes with your help, see if they can use their looking skills to make letter shapes – draw over faint dots you've made etc.
- From a stage of 'copying over' comes a stage of 'copying beneath'. Your child might be able to copy a single word underneath one you have written – keep the letters large and allow plenty of space.
- Early writing will not necessarily be the correct way up or stay in a horizontal line.
- Some children are still sorting out which hand to use in their writing.
- You can never have too much paper – keep a constant supply of scrap paper on hand.
- Children will be able to 'read' you what they are writing, though it will change from moment to moment.

There are a number of basic skills that a child requires if they are to master the art of writing. The following bullet list indicates the range required.

- Being able to hold and control a pen is a key motor skill that the child must be able to master. The issue of left- and right-handedness is not always straightforward but hopefully children will have a natural instinct for one hand or the other.

- A child has to be able to form letters, including making the distinction between upper and lower cases.
- To know the importance of letter formation directions is often very difficult and early errors tend to include a good deal of reversing of close pairings, e.g. b,d – p,q.
- Being able to write in a straight line and space out words is also an important skill in the learning of the shape of writing texts. It is the beginning of recognising that there are different ways to present texts.
- Punctuation is important to writing and not a more obvious feature, as it is not sounded out. Understanding that writing needs commas and full stops when there are pauses is the first step and those are the first punctuation marks to be considered.

Here are two theories of writing development that your students could look into. They might measure how usefully they track the development of writings that they collect from children in pre-school and in the early years of primary schools.

Theory 1: B. M. KROLL 1981

Kroll separated the development of writing into four stages.

Stage 1: PREPARATORY STAGE

Here, children master the basic motor skills needed to write and learn the basic principles of the spelling system.

Stage 2: CONSOLIDATION STAGE (age up to 6)

Children begin to write in the same way that they speak. Early writing makes use of short declarative sentences which include mainly 'and' as a conjunction. Such writing will also often feature incomplete sentencing as children don't know at this stage how to successfully finish off sentences.

Stage 3: DIFFERENTIATION STAGE (age up to 9)

Children become aware of the differences between speech and writing. They also begin to recognise the different writing styles that are available to them, e.g. a letter or a story. At this stage the writing will have lots of errors in it. Children at this stage will require lots of writing guides and frameworks to help structure their work. There should be the beginnings of a personal voice with writing being used to reflect thoughts and feelings.

Stage 4: INTEGRATION STAGE (12+)

Children develop their own personal styles and begin to understand that you can change your style according to the audience and purpose for which you are writing.

Theory 2: Dr CATHY BARCLAY 1996

Barclay proposes seven stages to a child's development in writing skills.

Stage 1: SCRIBBLING STAGE

A child will make random marks on a page. Whist doing this the child is likely to be speaking. This is an early indication of the link being made between speech and writing.

Stage 2: MOCK HANDWRITING STAGE

The child will begin to integrate writing with drawing. The development of a cursive 'writing' will appear. These rounded shapes are a forerunner to letters.

Stage 3: MOCK LETTERS

The letters that the child is producing are separate and increasingly distinctive.

Stage 4: CONVENTIONAL LETTERS

Barclay notes that most children are encouraged to produce their own names as first words. A child will usually put letters on a page but is able to read those letters as words.

Stage 5: INVENTED SPELLING STAGE

This is an interesting stage which really demonstrates the drive from the child to join in with the fun and system of writing. A child will spell in the way they understand the word should be spelt. This 'way' will often be entirely individual.

Stage 6: APPROPRIATE/PHONETIC SPELLING STAGE

This stage is where the child starts to attach spellings to the sounds that the written word is to represent. In English, of course, this phonetic spelling will involve lots of 'errors'.

Stage 7: CORRECT SPELLING STAGE

At this stage, a child will be able to spell most words accurately.

The teaching of reading and writing is a matter of great debate. In this respect, as I mentioned earlier, this is a help to your students in as much as it allows them scope to think about their own ways of making sense of this area. Students can measure the validity and usefulness of published research against the data that they can collect. The relationship between theory and practicality is one that your students are well placed to observe, having been in full-time education for some years.

Links with the personal investigation coursework are fairly clear. Students often choose to investigate child language acquisition, and the development of reading and/or writing is a clearly focused area that can be considered. The genuine sense of independent research and thinking that we hope to engender in our students has a real chance to thrive in this area of study.

Any of these theories can be employed to explore examples of children's writing. Beyond old exam paper and online resources, children's writing is not difficult to resource. Gather everything: your old school books, your children's, or writing by children of friends and family. Ask students to gather their own resources and very soon an impressive bank of children's writing will become the best resource you can imagine.

There are three texts below, with some explanation and some questions to enable exploration of children's writing. As ever, there is no attempt to be exhaustive here, more an indication of how you might start to explore these texts and others you bring to your classroom.

This is a text written by Molly, aged 4. It was her idea to write the letter.

Figure 14: Molly's letter (age 4)

With further exploration of Kroll's stages of writing development you can lead a discussion of whether Molly can be placed firmly in the preparatory stage or the consolidation stage of writing development. Is Molly simply acquiring the basic and fine motor skills needed to be able to function as a writer, as demonstrated by the inconsistent graphological features such as letter size and formation? Or is she well into the consolidation stage, as her writing demonstrates greater levels of sophistication than simply writing in short, declarative sentences? There are certainly elements of both stages. What else to explore?

- The conventions of letter writing: 'dear Uncle Village' and 'Love molly'.
- The social conventions of inviting someone for 'tee'.
- Letter formation: attempts at 'tails' on letter 'a', pen control to form letters 'y' and 'h'.
- Capitalisation and letter size: does the capitalised 'Please' demonstrate understanding of written grammar, even though there is no punctuation following the introductory phrase?
- Graphological features such as colour, use of kisses, size of 'Love molly' compared to the main body of the letter.
- What can we infer from the letter about the relationship between Molly and 'Uncle Village'? (One thing that cannot be inferred is the name. As you are aware, Nick Hall is one of the authors of this book. Molly is my friend's daughter and since her birth she has only ever heard me referred to as Village, an old childhood nickname.)

Answering a short essay question such as 'Explore what Molly's letter shows about early writing development' and selecting a bullet point or two from the list above will enable your students to be able to write about children's writing, as well as preparing them to be able to resource their own learning through the collection, analysis and explanations of their own and other children's texts.

Using texts written as part of formal education offers other insights in to children's writing development. Here is another text, written by one of the authors. This text, taken from an early school exercise book shows the expectations placed on young writers to create multi-modal texts. Multi-modality, even when this text was written in about 1980, is a dominant feature of writing by and for children. Illustrated stories, for children fortunate enough to be exposed to stories in the home, are an important part of making sense of early reading. It is, therefore, simple to make the link with early writing – pictures help readers and writers to make sense of stories.

Some initial question might help to frame the discussion of this and other texts.

- What does the text reveal about the relationships between writing and drawing?
- What does the text show us about linkage between social experience and writing development?
- How does teacher intervention affect writing development?
- What evidence is there for the development of grammatical understanding?

All of these questions, and more, can be explored in relation to just one text. By compiling a bank of texts it will be possible to extend discussions further, and to begin to weave theoretical perspectives in to discussions.

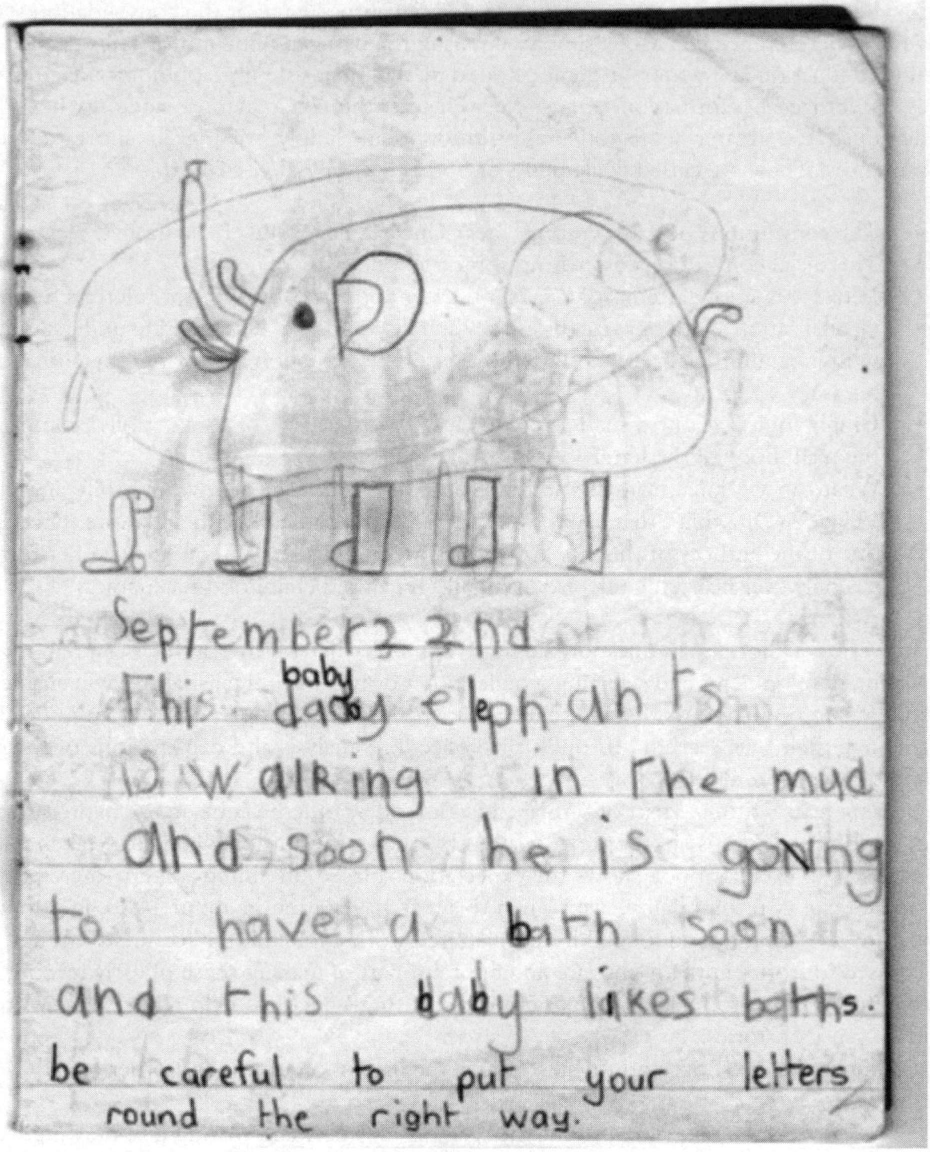

Figure 15: Illustrated elephant story (1980) – multi-modal text

With any texts you explore with students, always be mindful to avoid any kind of deficit model of reading children's texts. Always look to discover the development that is happening rather than what a child can't do yet.

Chapter 9

Language investigation

Project design

The language investigation coursework is in many ways the culmination of all of the students' learning on the course so far. It is also one of the most exciting moments for students and teachers. Students have the freedom to choose any area of language to research and analyse whilst you get the chance to watch your students independently demonstrate all of the skills that you have been helping them to acquire.

The most important decisions that you have to make during the production of coursework are when to offer help and when to give freedom to your students. High quality input from you at the earliest stages of coursework is vital: helping to structure ideas, develop methodologies and focus wandering minds is the best way to enable independent research.

By opening discussions of the possibilities that lie ahead of them at the earliest time possible in Year 13 you will plant the seed of investigation in your students' minds. By suggesting possible topics, particularly those outside of your exam board's specification, you can stimulate wide-ranging ideas. By allowing your students as much time as you can offer to develop fledgling ideas, you give yourself as much time as you can to hone and refine those ideas into sophisticated investigations.

At this stage you are essentially enabling students to write an introduction to their project. Requiring them to submit a few hundred words to a deadline is important once you have shared in some initial wonderings. Ask them to include thoughts on the background to their study, their motivations for choosing a particular area of research. They should also be able to frame a research question at this point, or a working hypothesis. Finally, they may be able to suggest some aims that underpin their research. This piece of writing needs to be well-crafted, concise and considered. It is also a draft that will inevitably need to be changed as the project develops. After all, you can't introduce a person you have never met, nor can you introduce a project you haven't undertaken. By reassuring your students that all research projects change at various stages and various ways and that this can be a virtue, will motivate them to get started.

Methodology

The next few pages take you through different methodological approaches that can be considered by you and your students in the early stages of designing their investigation. Each project has different methodological considerations and each methodology has different implications for the researching student.

There are two main sources of data that can be acquired or generated by research: written and spoken. Written data can be collected from a variety of sources. Printed and electronic sources are the primary sites for discovering interesting written texts. For students interested in the history of the representation of children in fiction, voice in online discussion fora or the relationship between readers and writers in guidebooks for walkers, written data is readily available. Churches and graveyards, railway stations and airports, billboards and bus stops are further sources of fascinating written data. Readymade spoken language is available too. Film, television and radio are rich sources and are even more readily available now that broadcasts can be downloaded and played on-demand so easily. Good examples which would bear rich research fruit might include: a study of the representation of the BNP in primetime media; a comparative study of the language of comedy on radio and television; or research into the relationship between character and discourse in the 'Die Hard' series of films.

Students can also devise investigations that generate new written or spoken data. A study of the development of writing skills between Years Four and Six of primary schools, or Years Seven and Nine of secondary schools can generate rich data. A student can devise a prompt or stimulus for writing and investigate the responses. Similarly, creating opportunities for recording speech can be rich too. Interviewing participants and recording responses to some visual prompts, recording peers in different social contexts or recording a teacher over a set time-period can generate some fascinating data, prime- for investigation.

Table 3: Planning grid

	01/10	08/10	15/10	22/10	29/10	05/11	12/11	19/11	26/11	03/12	10/12	17/12
Write Introduction	✓							✓	✓			
Plan and write Methodology	✓	✓						✓	✓			
Collect written data	✓	✓	✓									
Design interviews		✓	✓									
Record participants			✓	✓	✓							
Transcribe interviews			✓	✓	✓	✓						
Analyse data				✓	✓	✓						
Plan wider reading	✓	✓	✓									
carry out wider reading and notes	✓	✓	✓	✓	✓	✓	✓					
Write analysis						✓	✓	✓				
Seek advice on analysis					✓			✓	✓			
Write conclusion											✓	
Submit full draft											✓	
Collate folder									✓	✓	✓	✓

Because each investigation is different it is not possible to offer a structure that is applicable for every student. There is, however, a structure that can be personalised. The planning grid below serves many purposes. The model assumes that you are giving your students three months to complete the investigation. This is an intensive timeframe – you may choose to extend it. The visual impact of the grid has the effect of making students realise that they must multi-task throughout their research. They can't wait for one section to be completed before starting another. It also shows that some jobs need to be returned to. Furthermore, it forces students to realise that mini-deadlines are vital and need to be adhered to if the final deadline is to be met.

Data collection: Qualitative vs quantitative

The kind of data required is highly dependent on the investigation. The essential categories of data are qualitative and quantitative. It is fair to say that most of the data that is collected will be qualitative. This means that it can be measured, or analysed, for its qualities. For example a student might choose to measure the linguistic qualities of recipes through an investigation into the history of recipes. Or a qualitative study of children's writing might measure the graphological and grammatical differences of a cohort of Year Three students. This does not mean that the analysis is simply a personal reading of these texts however, nor does it mean that the results are merely impressionistic. Qualitative studies offer researchers the opportunity to discover findings from the data that they generate and to analyse these findings in the light of other researchers' investigations.

Quantitative data can be measured in terms of quantity. In small-scale research projects, like your students', this type of data can tend to be rather predictable, though we would never discount its relevance entirely. Questionnaires that require participants to respond to prompts on a scale from 'strongly agree' to 'strongly disagree' can be a valuable starting point for choosing what to follow-up in more detail. A simple and well-designed questionnaire to gather young children's views about writing might well inform an investigation into their writing skills. Our warning here, however, would be that in research projects on this scale, quantitative data is limited; its use should be restricted to informing the rich linguistic data that will form the bulk of the material for analysis.

Questionnaires

Questionnaires can take many forms. They can require a high level of commitment from participants if they expect prose responses to questions. They can result in simplified statistics if they use a sliding scale for respondents to offer their views. They can also result in lots of paper being used for little reward. Here are two suggestions that will allow your students to get the best out of the questionnaire format.

Questionnaire example one

Asking participants to agree or disagree with statements can be interesting. Look at the example below, taken from a questionnaire seeking views on televised Party political broadcasts.

My choice of who to vote for is influenced by Party political broadcasts

Strongly agree	Agree	Disagree	Strongly disagree

Rather than distributing lots of questionnaires with prompts like this and making pie charts with the results, advise your students to conduct oral questionnaires with fewer, hand-picked participants. The student can record the questionnaire and the transcribed conversation will be a much more revealing set of data than plain statistics. Note also the deliberate omission of a 'neither' category. By denying the participant the chance to avoid a positive or negative response the format stimulates discussion.

Questionnaire example two

A 'before and after' questionnaire can be a useful tool with which your students can seek further depth in the analysis phase of their research. If the study is investigating taboo language and its functions in Sixth Form discourse, a questionnaire might seek views on taboo language at a very early stage in the project. This initial questionnaire will then be very useful in designing subsequent research phases. If the next means of collecting data is covert recording of informal conversations, the student will now have two complementary data sets. A third set to add could be a follow-up questionnaire. Armed with transcriptions of recorded speech available to use as prompts in a conversation, the researcher could use a sliding-scale oral questionnaire, like the one above, to seek participants' views on actual instances of their use of taboo language.

Encourage your students to use questionnaires in ways that are closely linked to other means of data collection. They should form part of a cohesive data set that allows the analysis to be rich and deep. Examiners do not award marks for conducting hundreds of shallow questionnaires – they want to see your students' ability to investigate a precise area of language in depth.

Interviews

Interviews, like oral questionnaires, can be sources of rich data. In order to ensure that interviews generate reliable data that can be analysed as a data set rather than as a group of individual transcriptions, there needs to be some structure to the questions that are asked. Using a 'semi-structured interview' could allow your students to gain deep insight into a group of people's views.

Essentially, a researcher has a pre-written set of questions to ensure the interviews follow a standardised format. A researcher may choose to follow up any responses that are particularly interesting, or seek clarification of a response (hence 'semi-structured'). In a study on bi-lingualism in children, a semi-structured interview could be used to gain insight into parents' views on their children's language. A different interview could be used to gain the children's perspective. Though there may only be four interviews, when put alongside transcriptions of speech in different family settings, they could be very rich.

Transcriptions

Transcribing speech can be a laborious, time-consuming undertaking. One hour of speech takes between six and ten hours to transcribe. For your students that choose to investigate spoken language, the best advice that you can offer them is to spend time listening to data, carefully selecting rich moments to transcribe. It is within the researcher's remit to select which sections to transcribe, since it is their material. Listening is, furthermore, a far more revealing means of analysis than reading. It will allow them to hear intonation, emphasis, excitement, laughter and many other forms of meaning beyond those which are available when studying transcriptions. Your students only need enough transcribed speech to illuminate the points that are made in their analysis and conclusion. The full recordings can be submitted on CD or memory stick as evidence of the full recordings, should that evidence ever be required.

You can also make the process of transcribing data simple for your students by offering them a simple and standardised format. The easiest way to do this is to emulate the form of spoken data in transcriptions that your examination board uses in their exam papers. Here is a suggestion that will be enough to fulfil the demands of the language investigation coursework.

(.)   Pause
(3)   Numbered pause to indicate seconds
(...)   Unclear speech.
Key: (.) indicates brief pause

Ethical guidelines

There are important ethical considerations to make your students aware of before they undertake any data collection. The two areas to be clear about are consent and anonymity.

Your students must have very clear, written permission from all adult participants. Any data that is included in the study, be it a direct quotation, reference, inclusion in statistical details or appendix content must be made known to the participant. This is usually a simple process. If a participant is being interviewed, they can be asked to sign a form stating that they are aware of the purpose of the interview and how it will be used. The same process can be used when acquiring written data from participants. The only nuance here is when a student's methodology relies on secret recordings. In this instance, permission to include any data gained in this way must be sought retrospectively.

When children are used as participants, permission must be gained from their parents. The process is the same; a form must be signed and retained by the researcher as evidence of permission being given. With children even more so than with adults, it is highly risky, therefore best avoided, to collect data covertly.

Anonymity is also essential. All participants should be reassured that their identities will be concealed at the same time that permission is being sought. This can be simply done by changing the names of participants, locations, roles and any other information that would reveal identity. Although simple, it is still worth being very clear about how to respect this right when working on research projects in school. Students will be working in public areas where their data is visible to other students, so ensuring that they are each conscious of upholding their responsibility to act as professionally as they can, will help prevent any possible problems.

Analysis

Having done all of the research design, data collection and analysis this section seems to be the simplest to teach. Though it sounds simple, all the students have to do now is write up their findings. When all of the data has been explored your students should find themselves with lots of notes, annotated transcripts and texts, highlighted articles and small sections of analytical writing that they have been producing throughout the project. Now all they need to do is write it up.

Finding the balance between doing enough planning and finding excuses to stall writing is an art. There are steps that you can guide your students through in order to turn ideas and findings into analytical writing. Students need help to structure their work. It is best to think about the analysis as an entire, cohesive piece of writing that is broken into manageable sections to aid the reader. For some students selecting three or four linguistic categories is helpful. This can be the most relevant choice if the subject of study is young children's writing: each section of the analysis explains a particular type of development. In this instance, sub-headings like Lexical Development, Grammatical Development, Graphological Development and Awareness of Discourse could suffice. In other studies more pertinent categories might emerge and I would encourage students to consider how they could create headings that are unique to their study. Or, as another example, a comparison of different news broadcasters' presentations of conflict might generate categories such as Allied Forces, 'The Enemy' and BBC vs ITV. Using categories like these demonstrates a keen understanding of the material being analysed and can stimulate more engaging writing. In this instance, some students may need a reminder to continue to focus closely on linguistics and to use correct terminology.

Finally, this coursework will be a demonstration of development from AS studies. This means that all of the skills gained studying language in Year 12 should be employed in increasingly sophisticated ways. Considered explanations of contextual influences on meanings are needed. A fluent and confident academic tone should be used. Writing should be confident in its deployment of linguistic terminology and your students should be writing from the perspective of expert. All of this will set them up perfectly to return to their original question, which can be answered in the conclusion.

Conclusion

This is the final opportunity for the student researchers to demonstrate what they have learned from their study. They need to answer the question that they initially set themselves, concisely, and in a way that ties together the different sections of the analysis. It is as though the writing of the conclusion that they will be able to take a step back from all that they have achieved. Once they are able to do this, and see the project in its entirety, they will be able to answer the question that has driven their work for the previous months.

The other demand that needs to be fulfilled by their conclusion is reflective writing. As well as demonstrating an overall understanding of the data, the conclusion also needs to demonstrate understanding of the process. So evaluation of the choices that were made to complete the project will be valuable material here too. You may need to steer some students away from simply stating what went well and what they would do differently. These are excellent starting points, but only if they are pursued by the question 'why?'. When a student is able to fully explain how a particular research methodology allowed them to find rich data that opened up new and exciting lines of enquiry and understanding, then they are ready to conclude their coursework.

Media text

During the production of the coursework you need to be planting the seeds of thought about how the second part of the portfolio will be created. This part of the portfolio is a text that could be published in today's media, either online, in print or a spoken text. Using the broad research area as a starting point, your students need to create a media text designed for a non-expert reader. The options here are very wide. By encouraging your students to think as broadly as possible you can begin to ensure that they compose an original piece.

The text that they construct is your students' final opportunity to demonstrate talent as expert writers. The required skill is to convert subject knowledge gained in their role as researcher into a form that would interest and inform a non-specialist audience.

Table 4: Suggested ideas

Language investigation	Media text
How are gender and parental influence represented in primary age siblings' writing?	Article for local newspaper 'Siblings: A Classroom Secret?'
How do advertisers exploit linguistic devices to promote lifestyle of beauty in television adverts?	Magazine article entitled 'Because You're Worth It.'
Does a politician's ideological leaning affect their use of rhetorical devices?	Blog for www.americablog.com about British political rhetoric, allowing a more colloquial and opinionated view.
Does pet owners' speech to their animals reflect identified features of Child Directed Speech?	Humorous article for online magazine advising pet owners how to talk to their animals.

This table is offered for the purposes of suggesting relationships between an investigation and the media text; it is not an exhaustive list. Your specification will offer more precise advice, and coursework moderators are always around to help decide on projects.

Finally, this element of the course is designed to bring out the best in the students. If they are supported through the planning, design, research and writing stages of the project they will produce work that can impress both you and the examiners. This will become more possible if they are given lots of freedom to explore the ways in which linguistics plays a part in their world.

Concluding remarks

Cumulatively, these suggestions are about developing your capabilities in leading students through the course that you will design for them. You are helping your students to become thoughtful, resourceful and reflective learners.

During Year 12, students need to investigate the appropriate frameworks and terminology with which to study language. Their interest needs to be engaged in looking at how language operates and changes everyday in the society around them. In Year 13, you can create opportunities for these new-found skills to be honed through their application in investigation and research.

Please re-arrange, embellish and replace the ideas and activities as you see fit. Hopefully what you have read here will leave you fully prepared to adapt to the needs of curricular changes – which will inevitably come around. Your core understanding of what A level language study is will outlive many a new specification.

Enjoy.

Bibliography

Beeton, I. (2006) *Book of Household Management*, London: Wordsworth Editions Limited.

Cawdrey, R. (2006) *The First English Dictionary*, Oxford: The Bodleian Library.

David, E. (1960) *French Provincial Cooking*, London: Penguin.

Feinnes, W. (2001) *The Snow Geese*, London: Random House.

Floyd, K. (1987) *Floyd on France*, London: BBC Books.

Glasse, H. (1998) *The Art of Cookery made Plain and Easy*, Carlisle Massachusetts, US: Applewood Books.

Graves, R. (1960) *Goodbye to All That*, London: Penguin.

Hawthorne, N. (2007) *The Scarlet Letter*, London: Penguin Classics.

Hesse, H. (1985) *Autobiographical Writings*, London: Triad/Panther Books.

Jaffrey, M. (2003) *Ultimate Curry Bible*, London: Ebury Press.

Johnson, R. (2006) *An English Dictionary*, London: Penguin Classics.

Mandela, N. (2002) *Long Walk to Freedom* (vol. 1), London: Abacus.

Robson, B. (2005) *Farewell but not Goodbye*, London: Hodder and Stoughton Limited.

Scott, R. F. (2008) *The Journals of Captain RF Scott*, Oxford: OUP.

Seacole, M. (2005) *The Wonderful Adventures of Mrs Seacole in Many Lands*, London: Penguin Classics.

Slater, N. (2000) *Appetite*, London: Fourth Estate Limited.

Trevor, W. (2003) *The Story of Lucy Gault*, London: Penguin.

Index